TIES THAT BLIND

AN ALL-AMERICAN STORY

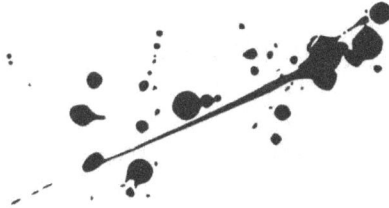

June Stephenson, Ph.D.

Other Books by June Stephenson
Tyrants in Our Time: Lives of Fourteen Dictators
Murder, The Only Way Out
The Lost Son
The Swedish Satchel
A Puppy's Tell-all Tale
My Three Cents' Worth
The Administrator
Sticks and Stones Are the Easy Part
It's All Right to Get Old
Women's Roots
A Lie is a Debt
Womankind
Innocent Weapons
Humanities Search for the Meaning of Life
The Two-Parent Family Is Not the Best
Men Are Not Cost-Effective

ACKNOWLEDGEMENTS

I am appreciative of the encouragement, the interest, and the suggestions from the following friends and family in the writing of this book:

Pansy Gordon	Nancy Bailey
Harriet Cavaglieri	Vickii Ellis
Alberta Wirtz	Terri Feathers
Charles Cahey	Rob Pinkston
Evelyn Smith	Janis Bailey
Amanda Smith	

Most especial appreciation
to Maureen Daly, retired
Deputy Attorney General
for the State of California, for
her legal assistance.

Last but not least, many thanks to my computer guru, Ted Nguyen for his valuable work on all aspects of the book's presentation.

June Stephenson

PART ONE

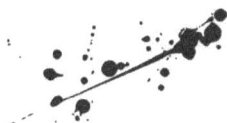

THE CRIME

STACEY AND JOSH

"Hey, Dude," the twelve-year-old boy called to the truck driver, "there's a baby in that dumpster. Don't dump that garbage in your truck. Hold it! Hold it! There's a baby in that dumpster."

Not hearing the boy's voice over the noise of his truck, the driver drove it closer to the dumpster. The other boy banged on the truck door.

"Stop, stop."

When both boys banged on the truck door, the driver leaned out the window. "You kids get away. I don't want to hit you. Go on to school."

"There's a baby," they both shouted, "a baby in the dumpster."

"A baby?" The driver turned the motor off and stepped down to the street. "A baby?"

"Yeah. Come on," they urged. The three walked quickly the few feet back to the dumpster.

"How you know about a baby?" the driver asked.

"We seen it."

"Alive?"

"No. No. It's dead." The boy quickly added, "but we didn't touch it. Honest."

The driver stood at the dumpster, and looking at its height asked, "How you kids get in that?"

"I stand on Devon's shoulders and jump in, and then I lean over and pull him up."

They watched the driver hoist himself over the side. "I see it," he called to the boys. He held up a bundle, a towel half-way covering it. When he lowered himself to the street, the boys pushed close to him.

"It's a boy," they said in unison, and then remained quiet.

"It's so little," one of the boys said.

"And a funny color," the other said.

"It's blue 'cause…" the driver started to explain and then he changed his mind. "I have to call the police. You kids go on now."

He opened the truck door and set the bundle carefully on the driver's seat, covering it with the dirty blanket. When he pulled his cell phone from his pocket the two boys just stood looking at the closed truck door.

"You kids go on." When they started to move away from the truck the driver asked, "What's your names? I have to give your names to the police so they can find you. May want to ask you some questions."

The boys looked at each other, shrugged, gave the driver their names which he wrote on a messed-up piece of paper. The boys walked away slowly as though reluctant to leave their discovery behind.

Later in the morning the school principal offered the meeting room to the cop where he interviewed the boys separately.

"Now go slowly," the cop advised Devon, the first boy interviewed. "The garbage truck driver said you and your friend, what's his name?"

"Elijah," Devon barely whispered.

"Don't be afraid," the cop urged. "Tell me what happened this morning."

"We... got in the dumpster..."

"Why? Did you know something was in there?"

"Had you seen someone around that dumpster? Maybe throw something in?"

"No. Oh, no. We was there just to get some..."

"What? Get some what?"

Devon looked down at the top of the table. "Food. We was hungry."

It was quiet for awhile before Devon was asked, "Did you find... food?"

"No, because we found the baby."

"How did you know it was a baby?"

"We didn't at first. Just something weird to be in with all that lettuce and carrots, and smashed up tomatoes. I just saw a cloth, like a towel, and pulled on it, and a baby rolled out."

"What did you do?" the cop repeated.

"We just wanted to run... tell someone. It was so small. I never seen a white baby before."

"What did you do?"

"We... I picked it up and Elijah wrapped the towel around it. When we heard the truck, I dropped it and we jumped out so we wouldn't get thrown in that big truck and hauled to the dumps."

"You got scared?"

"Sure did. I dropped the baby and jumped out 'a the dumpster and ran to where Elijah was banging on the driver's door. We was scared he was going to just dump that baby out in the garbage dump..."

"It's all right, son. You did a good thing, you boys. You did a good thing."

A few minutes later, convinced, after speaking separately to Elija, the cop decided the boys had no knowledge of who the baby belonged to, nor any knowledge of how it got in the dumpster. He drove back to Motel Six, and parked by the yellow crime scene tape.

———

Just twenty-four hours before that, the woman who had given birth to the baby in this Motel Six in a somewhat run-down section of South San Francisco, had called her boyfriend's cell phone in the Stanford athletic men's locker room. Annoyed, he picked the phone out of his locker where he had just stuffed his school clothes before suiting up in his football uniform. He listened a minute, then whispered into the phone, "Why are you the calling me now? I'm just going out on the field..."

"Josh, honey, we've got to go. They've started... the pains. Come pick me up. I've got stuff ready to..."

"You said September... September, you said. That's two months from now I can't go now. Must be a mistake. Honey, I've got spring practice."

"Josh, come. Don't talk...Please come right now..." Josh heard a groan.

After a long, silent moment he told her, "I'm coming. You be out on the curb. Gotta' change my clothes. I'll be there. "

He changed quickly into his jeans and cotton shirt , folding his football uniform and putting it into his locker, closed the metal locker door quietly, not banging it shut with a loud clang.

He drove leisurely over the paved tree-lined campus roads, watching the students going to their summer-school classes with friends. Though class work was "business as usual", as in autumn, winter, and springtime quarters, those during summer were more relaxed. The professors even seemed more friendly.

When Josh reached the student residence area and saw Stacey standing on the curb in front of her dorm, he was shocked back to the reality of the day. Stacey looked frightened. He accelerated and then slammed on his brakes as she rushed into his car, throwing her tote bag onto the floor. Immediately she doubled over.

Josh watched while the car idled. "You be all right for this ride?"

"Just hurry," she murmured.

Josh revved the motor.

Breaking speed limits, with his eyes on the lookout for traffic cops, Josh drove down Palm Drive, the main thoroughfare through the Stanford campus, and then after a few more turns, through Palo Alto, onto highway 101 north toward San Francisco. Stacey remained slumped beside him through most of the half hour trip, spasmodically groaning with pain.

"Are you sure about this?" he asked, bewildered.

"It has to be. It's early I guess."

"Two months?" he asked.

As the next pain gathered momentum she sucked in her breath and gritted her teeth, wanting passionately to yell, but she didn't.

A bit after two o'clock in the afternoon they pulled up to the reception driveway of Motel Six in South San Francisco, a motel they had picked months before, one on the busy highway with few cars in front, which meant few customers.

They had carefully planned it. Now with the almost unbearable pains, Stacey's fervent wish was to let go with a curdling scream, or do anything that would stop the pains that kept coming, one on top of the other.

Josh stopped his car in the archway, left the motor running, got his credit card out of his wallet, ran to the reception desk, held the card out to the clerk, signed the registration pad, and grabbed the room key extended to him.

"Thank God," he said, jumping back in the car, glancing at Stacey who was so white he wondered for a moment if she were alive. "We have an end room," he said trying to find something good to say.

In one of the few moments without pain he helped Stacey out of the car, into their room, and onto the bed. When the pains started again she covered her head with the blankets.

Josh was helpless. "I'm sorry, honey. Really sorry" he said. "Maybe we should go to a hospital..."

"No. No. We agreed. I'll do this. We'll do this. It won't take... long."

But it took nine hours.

Josh did what he could, massaging Stacey's hands, wiping her forehead with a towel.

Long after dark, water flowed out of Stacey's body soaking the bed, followed by a little blood, and then the head of a brown-haired baby.

Josh panicked when he thought the head was stuck, but with Stacey's final push, the whole body came out, flailing its arms and making a noise which they both recognized with a sidelong glance at each other, was the first noise of a newborn baby entering the world.

Without stopping to help Stacey, Josh took the scissors she had placed on a towel by the bed as they had rehearsed, cut the umbilical cord, covered the baby's face with the towel, and held it until there was no more sound nor arm movement. He rolled the baby in the towel, did not look at Stacey and murmured, "I'll be right back."

And he was. He was surprised to see Stacey up and in the bathroom.

"You're up?"

"I can make it back before anyone gets up. Sarah is gone for the week-end."

Josh drove the twenty-five miles to the campus, numb to the morning traffic, Stacey's head rested on Josh's shoulder, her eyes wide open but not seeing. On the campus, she let herself into the empty lobby of her dormitory, crept up the stairs, and opened her door. She pulled the bedspread down, fell sound asleep on top of her blankets and didn't stir until she felt someone rousing her with a gentle hand on her hip.

"Stacey?" she heard her dorm's student-advisor, Kate, through the haze of waking up. "I knocked several times."

"There are a couple of men here who say they need to talk with you." Stacey tried to sit up, but waited until the man nearest her could help. Taking a wallet from his inside jacket pocket, he held out a badge and introduced himself as a policeman from South San

Francisco. The other man, also holding a badge said, "Police, Palo Alto."

"Stacey Hodgkins," the first man said, looking at a paper in his hand to ensure himself or her name "we need to ask you some questions."

Dazed, Stacey looked at the three people in her room.

"Where were you last night?" she was asked.

"Where was I? I was... I was here."

"Is that true?" the man asked Kate.

"No."

"So," the other man said, pleasantly, "why don't you tell us where you were last night."

Stacey couldn't find any words.

The man continued, softly, "Were you with your boyfriend?"

She nodded.

"His name is... what?"

"Josh," she whispered.

"His last name?" He wrote Stacey's answer in a small note pad.

"Where were you?"

She started to cry, burying her face in her blanket.

"Stacey," he explained, "I need to read you your rights about answering. You don't have to answer my questions, but you should know that if you do, what you say could be held against you if what happened last night goes to trial. And you can have an attorney.

If you can't afford one, an attorney will be provided for you. Do you understand that?"

Stacey said, "Yes."

"You drove to South San Francisco to a motel?" he asked.

Stacey didn't answer, her body shaking with soundless sobs. He continued questioning.

"You went to the Motel Six?" His voice had lost its pleasantness.

"I don't know the name," she said.

She wished he would stop. Her stomach hurt and her head throbbed. "And you had a baby?"

She sat rigid. Her tears stopped. "Yes," she said, as though it had just occurred to her. "Yes, I had a baby."

"We would like you to answer a few more questions. Would you be willing to do that?"

"Yes."

"The baby was male or female?"

She shook her head, "I don't know."

"Did you look at it?"

"No."

"What did you do with it?"

"I don't know."

"Did your boyfriend do something to it?"

"I don't know."

"What did your boyfriend do with it?"

"I don't know," she said, crying again into the blanket.

He noticed the sheet covered with blood and called to his sergeant, "Call an ambulance. She's hemorrhaging."

Stacey was hurriedly carried to the ambulance and rushed into the emergency entrance of a hospital where she was immediately administered medications. When she woke there was a policewoman sitting in her room. She summoned the man who had questioned her in her dormitory room, and announced that Stacey was awake and alert. He entered the room and read to her:

"Stacey Hodgkins, age 20, currently residing at Toyan House, Stanford University, California, you are being arrested for the murder of infant 'John Doe' in conspiracy with Josh Stockman, 20, a resident of Sigma Chi Fraternity House, Stanford University, California, the murder occurring at approximately one a.m., July 14, 2002 at Motel Six, 22795 Highway 101, room 2119, South San Francisco, San Francisco County, California."

The cop explained to the policewoman the hospital would be delineated as a 'prison hospital room,' until the suspect would be well enough for transfer to San Francisco jail to be held for arraignment. He ordered that the policewoman must be in the room at all times until the prisoner would be moved under guard.

———————

Josh climbed the stairs in the fraternity house on the Stanford Campus to his room he shared with two other sophomores who were just then getting out of bed, heading for their showers down the hall. They kidded Josh about staying all night with Stacey for the first time.

"Must have been one hell-of-a-night," Scott suggested, he and Leo raising eyebrows at each other.

Josh returned a half-smile, hoping to convey that things were as Scott intimated. They both took their towels and left the room. Josh in solitude and privacy lay down on the top of his bed and was soon snoring, pulling deeply for air.

He woke to see a man sitting on his bed, his face not ten inches from his own.

"You Josh?"

"Who the hell are you?"

"Police." He held out his identification, as did his partner.

Josh sat up "You can't come in here..."

The policeman rose from the bed. "Where were you last night? How come you're sleeping with your clothes on? "

Josh shuddered, cautioned himself to keep quiet, yet couldn't resist showing he knew his rights. "You got a warrant? You can't come in here... "

"Don't tell me what I can or cannot do. Look, you need to come down to the police station with us. We need to get things on the record."

"On the record? What, for instance?

"Murder, for instance." Then he cautioned Josh. "Hold on a minute. Take it easy. You have the right to remain silent. Anything you say can be used against you if this goes to trial. You have a right to an attorney, and if you cannot afford one, one will be appointed for you at no cost. Knowing and understanding your rights as I have explained them, are you willing to talk to me without an attorney present?"

"Yes, I understand. But why would there be a trial when I didn't do anything?"

"Josh, you do understand what I just said?"

"Yes."

"And that you can have an attorney, and if you can't afford one, one can be provided with no cost to you?"

"Yes, but I'll get one - a good one."

"Murder?" he questioned himself. Had he hit someone on the freeway and not known it? "Officer, you've made a mistake. I don't know what you're talking about."

"You will. Come on. Let's go."

Josh hesitated. "If I refuse?"

"We will get an arrest warrant, and you will have to come with us anyway. Just make it easier on yourself, okay?"

Josh dressed and left with the officers.

At the police station he was ushered into a small room by the two men who woke him, while another man in uniform was setting up a tape recorder. Josh's mind was racing. What did these men know about last night? He had cleaned up that motel... left no identification... scrounging in dumpsters? ...maybe some homeless...looking for food. But he remembered, what he threw in the dumpster was wrapped. No one would mistake that for food. Maybe something else had happened and he is being confused with somebody else. Sigma Chi men, he thought, being the party-boys on campus, frequently got into trouble making out with some girl where they shouldn't be.

Once the three were seated on the hard wooden chairs the questions started, "Why were you in South San Francisco last night?"

"Who says I was?"

"You did. You gave your credit card to the clerk at Motel Six." Josh fumbled through his wallet and brought out his credit card.

"I have it right here."

"Your number is on his registration."

"Oh. So... what if it was?"

"Who were you with?"

"Would you tell me why I'm here? I need to make a phone call. I think... don't I get to make a phone call?" He fumbled for his cell phone.

"Who you going to call?"

"My father."

"Where's he?"

"Evanston, Illinois."

"Use your cell phone. Put it on 'speaker'."

Josh dialed, noticing his hands were shaking. He turned his back on the men so they wouldn't see his nervousness.

"Mom. I need to talk to Dad. Is he home?"

From his cell phone speaker the whole room heard a woman's voice.

"Yes. What is it Josh? Are you all right?..." She called out, "Charlie. it's Josh on the phone. He sounds terrible."

Into the phone she told Josh his father was coming.

"Hello, son," a hearty male voice boomed. "How come a Saturday morning call. Lucky I'm not still sleeping." He laughed a big laugh.

Josh hesitated, not sure what to say. "Dad... I need the home phone number of Jack Shaughnessey. Could you get it? "

"Good God, boy. The busiest attorney in San Francisco and just like that you want his home phone number. What the hell is the matter?"

"I can't explain right now... If you give me his number, then he can tell you..."

"No way in hell am I going to do that. If you're in trouble you come on home, let me take care of it. What did you do anyway?"

Quietly Josh explained, "Dad, I don't think this is something you can take care of. I need to talk to..."

"Josh, I'm coming out there. Just keep your mouth shut. I don't know what you did, but there's nothing we can't fix, son. Just don't talk to any of your frat buddies. I'll catch a plane this afternoon. See you tomorrow morning. Whatever it is, don't talk to anybody. That's an order." He slammed the phone down. "Damn. "

No sooner had Josh shut down his cell phone than it rang. He answered it before the police told him not to, then they let him continue, though once again they asked him to put it on 'speaker.'

"Hi, honey."

"Mom? What are you doing, why are you whispering?"

"Your dad went back out to the yard. I have Jack Shaughnessey's phone number, his home phone. Jane and I are friends you know. Here's their number." Josh reached across the table for a pen and paper and wrote the number, tore the piece of paper, folded it and started to put in his pocket when the police took it from his hand. His mother continued on the phone. "You know they live in Burlingame. I have to hang up. Your dad is coming back in the house. I love you, honey. I'll find out what this is all about when I call Jane. Bye."

"Who is Jack Shaughnessey?" Josh was asked.

"An attorney friend of my father's."

"Then that is somebody else you can call. Yes, a suspect can call an attorney."

"What am I a suspect of?"

"Murder. Are you waiving your rights?"

"I don't know about that. I just want to know why I'm here."

"You're here because you are being held as a suspect for murder."

"What murder? I didn't murder anyone. I'm a suspect?"

"Yes. You are a suspect. We are arresting you for the murder of a 'John Doe' in San Francisco County Motel Six, on July 14, 2002, in conspiracy with a Stacey Hodgkins."

Josh stood up, red in the face, "I didn't murder anyone. That baby was dead. You can't murder anyone who is dead."

"You have been arrested. You will be arraigned tomorrow in court." The policeman reached under the table, pressed a button, and almost immediately another policeman came into the room, took Josh's arm and walked him out of the room.

At Motel Six in South San Francisco, the sergeant and his assistant prepared to question the clerk at the registration counter. It went as they suspected it would. "May we see your check-in sheet?" the sergeant's assistant asked the clerk. The two policemen scanned the list.

"This couple, Mr. and Mrs. Jerry Smith, what did they look like?"

"I didn't pay no attention. I didn't see the woman. She stayed in the car when her boyfriend registered. I remember that he was in a terrible hurry. Maybe he had another date later on," he laughed a humorless laugh. "Or maybe this was going to be his first time."

"You didn't think they were married?"

"No. You can tell. I watched them go into their room. No luggage. But we don't snoop."

The sergeant said, "We need the number of the credit card and the car license number, and a description of this guy," he looked at the register, "Jerry Smith."

"Sure." And as the clerk was writing the information, he told the policemen he didn't get the car license number. He had meant to go down to the room and get it off the car but another couple came in and he forgot about the car.

"What make was it. Can you describe it?"

"No. I didn't look. The guy was in a hurry."

"And what did 'the guy' look like?"

"I don't know. Awfully young. Like maybe seventeen or eighteen maybe. Nothing special."

"Black?"

"Hell, no. Niggers don't spend on sex."

The police exchanged a glance. One said quietly to the other, "the baby was white."

"What baby?" the clerk wanted to know.

"That couple had a baby in that room, dumped it in that dumpster. It was white - so that couple was white." "We'd like to see the room."

"It's not been cleaned yet. We're short of help..."

"All the better. Let's go."

ADELE

Stacy's mother, Adele, was doing a typical Midwestern thing when the phone rang that Thursday morning in July in her suburban home in Evanston, Illinois. With her straw hat and garden gloves she was a picture for *House and Gardens* as she cut off the deadhead roses on one of the 79 rose bushes in her garden, the most beautiful in a five block radius.

"Stacey. Why are you calling? Why aren't you... isn't this one of the days you have a study group for your finals? Honey, are you sick?"

"No, Mom...but, Mom. Can you come out? I can't... only have ten minutes I can talk... Mom..." Her crying smothered the words she tried to say.

"Stacey, if you can't talk, is there someone else there I could talk to... to tell me what's wrong." Stacey handed her cell phone to the police woman in her hospital room, mumbling, "would you tell my mother... what's... going on, please."

"Ma'm," the policewoman said into the phone, "are you there? Good. Your daughter is in a hospital because she was hemorrhaging, but she is going to be all right.... no, she was not in an accident... No... she delivered a baby. M'am, are you still there? M'am? Yes. Yes, she was pregnant. M'am... You say you didn't know... The baby? No Ma'm, it didn't. Wait, she wants to talk to you."

Stacey took back the phone and asked once more if her mother could come out to Stanford.

Stumbling to talk, Adele assured her daughter, "As soon as I can make arrangements for Maggie and Bobby, I'll be there Honey."

"Mom. Don't tell Dad."

"I won't, Honey."

JOSH AND JACK SCHAUGHNESSEY

Before his arraignment, Josh was housed temporarily in a city jail cell in Palo Alto until arrangements could be made to transfer him to San Francisco County, the crime's locale. He refused food, and slept off and on as though afraid to let go. When the noise in the office woke him even before daylight, he sat on the edge of the bed, his head in his hands unable to clear his thoughts.

He knew what he and Stacey had done, but couldn't see it all as reality. They had rehearsed it many times and had done it exactly as they had planned, yet it was as though they had yet to go through with it. For a brief moment he let himself think maybe they hadn't done it yet, and that he wasn't sitting in a jail cell.

At that point the guard was telling Josh his attorney was coming to see him. Then Josh remembered calling Jack Shaughnessey, who was just then being let into his cell. He jumped up.

"Uncle Jack! Oh my God." He hugged the old-time friend of his family as he burst into pent-up tears. Jack patted Josh on the back, saying, "We frat boys help each other, remember? We'll get to work on this, Josh. I'm meeting your prosecutor," Josh backed away, not having heard that word before related to him, "we'll see what he's got. I only have a few minutes for now. Wanted to let you know I'm here. We go before the magistrate at ten o'clock. You be okay?"

"Yes. I am now that you're here."

Jack called out to the guard to get a private conference room for Josh and himself.

After they were settled Jack asked Josh, "Tell me what you did last night." When Josh was finished Jack asked him for the second time, "You're sure there was no sign of life from the baby when it was born."

Josh didn't hesitate. "I'm sure."

"Like I said, I have to see what the prosecutor has, but when we're before the judge you must remember don't volunteer anything. Answer questions from the judge as simply as you can. This is going to be tough. I'm pretty sure we'll get bail, but sometimes... well, you just never know. Tell me this. If the baby had been born alive, what did you and Stacey plan to do with it?"

"We were...Can I say, well,...Can I say we were going to, we had heard we could leave it at the fire station and nothing would be said. Can I say that?"

"Yes. If it's true."

"Hmm." Jack stood up to leave and explained to Josh, "you'll be driven up to San Francisco to the courthouse there. I'll see you there. Answer the questions but don't elaborate. They know you were at that Motel Six and other things. No time now. Don't talk to anyone about this matter unless I am present. Goodbye Josh." They hugged. "See you later today. We'll do okay."

Josh was driven to the Superior Court of San Francisco County, California, given an orange jumpsuit. His hands were cuffed and tied to his belt. He was led into the courtroom, when he felt his knees shake and he was dizzy. He realized he hadn't eaten for hours and had barely slept.

He looked at the huge courtroom, like the ones he had seen on *"Law and Order,"* when he immediately spotted Jack Shaughnessey seated at a table, and was relieved when the policeman sat him down next to Jack. Across the aisle, Josh noticed a man he had not seen before who was scanning people coming into the courtroom. His eyes rested on Josh who looked away.

When everyone in the room was seated, including the many spectators, the room remained quiet for about ten minutes. Then when the door to the judge's chambers opened, the bailiff announced: "Please rise." The judge walked into the courtroom and seated herself in her chair when the bailiff announced, "The Honorable California Superior Court Judge of San Francisco County, Wilma Woodward."

After the bailiff asked the assemblage to be seated, the judge announced, "This case is The People vs. Josh Stockman and Stacey Hodgkins, case number CR

0045892. Would all counsel identify yourselves for the record."

"Henry Cook for The People, Your Honor."

"Mark Collins representing Stacey Hodgkins. My client is confined to the hospital but was arraigned yesterday in San Francisco County, Your Honor."

"Jack Shaughnessey representing Josh Stockman, Your Honor."

As had been done with Stacey the previous day, Josh was told by the judge, "Joshua Arnold Stockman, you are charged in count one of violation of California Penal Code section 187, premeditated murder in the first degree of John Doe committed on July 14, 2002. As to the charge of murder in the first degree in count one, how do you plead?"

"Not guilty, Your Honor."

Josh's voice dropped when he heard a disturbance at the back of the courtroom. He turned around to see a large boisterous man pushing the door open. He recognized his father's voice and saw a man rushing toward the front talking loudly.

"Just a minute," the man shouted walking to the front of the court. "That's my son up there. What's going on here? Most respectful, your honor, but that's my son. What are you doing to him up there?"

Recognizing his old friend, Jack Schaughnessey, he called out, "Hey Jack, how'd *you* get here...I've been driving around like a bat out of hell trying to find my son. Plane got in at six. What a trip."

"Bailiff restrain that man and bring him up. What's your name?"

"Charlie Stockman and that's my son, Josh. Why's he got those orange cover-alls on?

"Mr. Stockman," the judge explained, "this is an arraignment. Your son is charged with murder. I must ask you to sit down or we will have to remove you from the courtroom."

Charlie did not sit down. He approached Josh before the bailiff could get to him and shouted, "What the *hell* did you do?"

"Dad. I had to do it. You wanted me to play football and..." He fainted.

The judge banged her gavel. "Court will adjourn until ten o'clock tomorrow morning. Counsel," she addressed the prosecutor, "bring the coroner's report. Bailiff, get the suspect to the health center."

Jack Shaghnessey, alarmed at what could be considered a confession by Josh, jumped up. "Your Honor, may we have a recess here so I may consult with my client when he comes to?"

After scanning her calendar, the judge banged her gavel. "This case is continued until August 3rd, a three week continuance."

CHARLIE

Josh's father, Charlie was an older father, forty-four years old when his first and only child was born to his third wife, Karen, who was twenty-three when they married. Charlie adored Karen whom he was courting when married to Denise. His hopes of marrying Karen were blocked several times. He had to convince her that his age would have no bearing on their marriage. He bragged about how strong he was, worked-out every day after playing golf, then swam in his club's pool for an hour.

Nevertheless Karen was concerned about the age difference, and also that he was still married to Denise. Still she was intrigued about being married to a multi-millionaire. She rationalized that she would probably not get a better offer.

The financials in Charlie's divorce from Denise were simple as there were no children. He deeded their house to Denise and settled a sizeable sum on her. They divorced amicably.

After their wedding Karen tolerated his adoration of her, especially the incessant photography sessions.

He couldn't seem to get enough of her, and especially after she told him she was pregnant. He never thought it would happen. He was used to his male friends kidding him about being sterile, after three marriages and no children.

Karen wrongly interpreted his reaction as something he did not want.

"Don't worry, sweetheart," she told him. "We don't have to have this. I don't really want a baby."

"What are you saying? Get rid of it? No way! *You* may not want a child but *I* do. I want what every man wants. I want a *son!*"

He hugged her so tight he hurt her swelling breasts. "Oh Baby, Baby, Baby. This is the happiest day of my life. You have given me everything."

———————

Josh Arnold Stockman, nine pounds eight ounces, was born eight months later. Karen dozed after the difficult night's work and woke up in her private hospital room overflowing with flowers, to a husband who couldn't stop kissing her.

When his son was handed to him, the squirming, screaming, red-faced newborn was as unhappy as his father was happy. Charlie kissed his son on the top of his head and declared, "This is the quarterback I would have been."

He adored his son as much as he adored his wife. To the woman who had done the most for him, he showered with gifts of which there seemed to be no limit.

And there was no limit either on the time he could spend with his little boy, as no employer required his presence, being retired from the drug manufacturer Geminich, which had just developed the most promising cancer cure there was. His commissions rolled in.

The hours he could spend with his son were endless as Josh grew, crawled, walked and then learned to run. There were times when Karen would admonish Charlie to limit the "play time," to not wear out their little boy, though Josh didn't complain. He liked seeing his daddy smile when he succeeded in putting one of his square wooden blocks in the square openings rather than in trying to force it into the circle.

Charlie was sure Josh was especially intelligent and had him tested when he was fourteen months. Charlie was right: Josh was exceptionally bright for his age.

In all his years Josh never disappointed his father, so his father never had to live through his own college football disappointment, again. When Josh was picked for the varsity football team at Stanford, though only a sophomore, his father literally cried with joy. When Charlie did not make the cut at Stanford when he was a junior, he buried his grief, and eventually, earned a

Masters of Business Administration Degree and concentrated on making money.

ADELE

Stacey's mother Adele didn't get away from her two younger children as soon as she had hoped. It was more difficult than she thought it would be to get her sister to stay at her house during the day although she had done so previously. Also Stacey's father was critical of his wife going off to Stanford every time Stacey "had a toothache," as he had said.

"Let her grow up," he'd say, only this time he was more insistent. "Besides it makes problems for me. Sometimes I have to stay at the office longer than usual, then I have to call Beth to stay at the house later."

"This time" Adele implored, "Stacey sounded almost hysterical. I need to go. Beth understands. I'll only be gone a week until Stacey settles down so she can get through her finals. It would be terrible for her to have to postpone them..."

"Go ahead, Hon." In the end he was always supportive after he made a protest. He didn't want Stacey to postpone her finals either, if that was even possible. He especially didn't want her to lose a whole quarter's worth of units after paying tuition and dorm fees. Better to let Adele make a quick trip and get Stacey back on track.

She landed at the San Francisco Airport, rented a car, set the cruise control at seventy, and arrived at the Palo Alto Hospital just before visiting times had expired. She inquired and found Stacey's room where she was met by a policewoman who frisked her. The police woman examined her purse, and requested proof of relationship with the patient. If Adele had not known the patient in bed was her daughter she would never have recognized her. She caught herself crying, standing away from the bed so Stacey would not see her distress.

Eventually she whispered to her sleeping daughter, "Stacey, I'm here."

Adele sat in a chair next to her daughter, waiting impatiently for her to wake up. The policewoman had said Adele could stay only twenty minutes, but that did not include Stacey's sleeping time.

Adele wanted to wake her up, talk awhile and see what she could do to get Stacey out of the hospital. Maybe try to get her back to her dorm. She didn't look sick. Was it true about a baby? That must have been confused with someone else. Maybe one of her dorm sisters had a baby?

Adele moved restlessly in her chair, anxious to talk, get things figured out, and then leave to get a motel room.

"Mom,...?" Stacey asked. "Oh, Mom. You came. Can you get me out of here. Take me home."

"That's what I want to do." Adele hugged her daughter, however uncomfortably by leaning half-way over the bed.

"The police lady says I have to go to court. How can I go to court when I can hardly stand up?"

"I'm going to talk to the doctor, honey. Tell me what happened? You were hemorrhaging, the nurse in the hall told me. Sometimes when we have our period we can't turn it off." She looked quizzically at the policewoman who was pretending to be reading.

The policewoman looked up from her book, read the question on Adele's face, and explained, "M'am, we're here to ensure that your daughter does not try to run away. She, as you must know, is a suspect in a crime and should be in jail, but her physical condition is such that she will..."

"Run away? A crime? What crime? That's impossible. Stacey, what is it they say you have done?"

"Killed a baby."

"Killed a baby! My God. On the highway? Where?"

Stacey might have answered, but at that moment the door to her hospital room opened, admitting a man with a briefcase. The policewoman rose when he announced, "I'm Mark Collins, court appointed attorney for," reading his folder," a Stacey Hodgkins. That's you?" he asked of Stacey who nodded.

"And you are?" he asked of Adele.

"I am Stacey's mother. Please can you tell me what's going on. What do they say Stacey did?"

"M'am, we should not talk with others in earshot. Meet me..." he handed Adele his business card. "M'am," he repeated to Adele, "Come to my office..." he fumbled through an appointment calendar, "tomorrow morning, nine-thirty." He checked his calendar again, "Yes, nine-thirty is clear." He wrote quickly on a card and handed it to Adele. "Okay. I have an appointment in twenty minutes. Glad I caught you Mrs.," looking at his folder, "Hodgkins. Goodbye Stacey. Get well so we can go to work." He was out the door almost running into the white-coated doctor entering the room. The policewoman waved the doctor in.

The doctor had not said a word to anyone when Adele rushed to him asking, "Please, doctor, can you explain what's going on? When can I take my daughter back to her dorm? Her finals start in two days."

"Stacey is well enough now to leave the hospital but she will not be going to her dorm. She will be transferred tomorrow to the San Francisco jail to wait for her arraignment."

"To the jail? To jail? Why?" she pleaded.

"I'm sorry I can't tell you more, I am in charge only of your daughter's health. I don't have answers for anything else. Sorry I can't help you. Stacey will be moved tomorrow morning. You can...do you know how to get in touch with Stacey's attorney, the man who just left here?"

"Yes," she looked at the card she still held in her hand. "Yes. I'll see him tomorrow at nine-thirty in his office." She turned to her daughter "Stacey, honey. You're not going to any jail. There's been a tremendous mistake. We'll get this cleared up tomorrow. I've got to go and check into a motel, and phone your dad to let him know you're okay. Then I'll be back here to be with you. I love you." She leaned over the bed to give Stacey a long hug. "Honey", she said, "Don't worry, I'll be back here as soon as I can."

"Mom," Stacey said softly, pleading. But her mother was already down the hospital corridor.

———————

The following day and with great effort in locating Mark Collins' office, Adele learned some of the particulars of Stacey's situation.

"Stacey and her boyfriend are accused of killing a baby," Mark Collins explained, "because, as Stacey told me, Josh told her having a baby did not fit into their plans for the future. Having it and giving it up for adoption, there was no way they could keep that information from you, nor could your daughter Stacey countenance an abortion."

"Of course not," Adele said. "That's murder."

Mark Collins wondered if Adele even heard what he was saying. Adele, who was crying, struggled to ask "Why didn't they just have the baby and get it adopted?"

"Mrs. Hodgkins, that's all in the past. Stacey was desperate that you not ever find out she was pregnant. She told me her mother would be so disappointed in her that she had sex before marriage that she wouldn't speak to her again. It would be like losing her mother."

Adele wailed. "She could have come to me. I would have taken care of it. She could finish school... "

"It's over. Stacey could not even imagine, as you say, 'coming to you.' "

Adele stopped crying suddenly. "Are you saying my daughter is afraid of me?"

Mark stalled. "Well, maybe not afraid... but not able to tell you. According to the police report the first thing she said when she was arrested was that her mother must never know."

"Oh my God. Oh my God! "

"They had it all planned. It's all in the police report. They were 'scared to death their parents would find out.' Abortion or adoption were out of the question. Not having their parents find out was their most important goal.'"

"Even Josh's parents?"

"Especially Josh's father. 'My father will kill me,' was what he said. ' Waited all his life to see his son get on the football team, and getting Stacey pregnant would knock that football dream to high heaven.'"

Adele's sobs quieted long enough for her to ask, "And what did Stacey say?"

"That her mother had so many plans for her, but then the police report read that Stacy mentioned something about maybe it wouldn't have been so bad if her mother could have seen the baby. The point is now we have to get busy and come up with a defense," Mark said, suddenly business-like. "We'll talk about that later this morning, after the arraignment."

"I know you said the arraignment is this morning, but what is it?"

"The time for the defendant to enter an initial plea."

"Can I take her to her dorm after that?"

"Not unless we can get bail. She is under arrest."

"Oh my God," Adele sobbed.

Mark Collins placed papers in his briefcase. "I have to be in court in five minutes. You can come with me if you wish." Still crying, Adele followed him out the door.

STACEY

The courtroom was crowded but quiet. Mark Collins put his briefcase noisily on the attorneys' table, and dragged his chair as he sat down. Every person in the room watched his movements until they were distracted by the noise of a woman who had entered the courtroom. She found one of the few places on a bench near the attorneys' table and standing, looked searchingly around the room. Adele who had no familiarity with a courtroom, was looking for her daughter among the spectators.

Soon a bailiff announced the arrival of the judge, and asked for the assemblage to rise. It was then that Adele saw Stacey standing next to Mark Collins. When the bailiff asked the court to be seated, Adele remained standing hoping to get Stacey's attention.

"Madam," the bailiff called to Adele, "please be seated. And don't attempt to make contact with the defendant."

At that, Stacey saw her mother. They waved at each other and cried. Mark pulled Stacey down to her chair and wrote something on a pad in front of her. She turned facing the bar and stifled her sniffles.

When the judge asked the prosecutor to present the people's case, a man at the table on the opposite side of the courtroom stood up to address the judge. "Your Honor, Mr. Stockman's defense counsel informed me this morning that he is being charged separately."

"And who is Josh Stockman's counsel?"

"John Shaughnessey, your honor."

"No, your honor. There is some confusion here. I was told by Mr. Collins that his client, Stacey Hodgkins, may wish to plead out and that her boyfriend may join his case with hers, but that is not settled."

Annoyed the judge announced, "I would like both counselors in my chambers." The judge rose and left the courtroom.

Their private session lasted 15 minutes. The judge returned to her seat and announced the proceedings would be continued two days from that date for further arraignments, when both attorneys would return with statement of pleadings.

Before leaving the courtroom, each attorney arranged for a private session for the next day with their clients. A meeting with clients and their parents was arranged two weeks from then.

JOSH AND STACEY

It had been a rush to get the four parents from Evanston, Illinois, and their attorneys to meet in the San Francisco jail conference room on the day required.

It was the first time Josh and Stacey had been together since that painful night, yet they made no eye contact. Nor did the parents who came from the same neighborhood, and attended many PTA and other school events as their children moved through the Evanston school system.

Stacey's attorney opened the discussion as to why they were all together, stressing that his client had indicated she did not want to endure a jury trial and would consider making a plea.

Josh stood up and said, loudly, "I am not making any plea. I didn't kill anybody."

Charlie Stockman shushed his son and pulled him down by the back of his jacket. "Don't make it worse than it is," he advised.

Josh pulled away from his father, but quieted.

"My job here," Mark Collins began to explain, "is to advise these two young people the legal consequences of their going to trial, or the legal consequences of their pleading guilty, avoiding a trial. The odds of their lesser sentence with a plea bargain are good. I'll explain."

"If these two young people go to trial, the state will ask for a jury trial. It will be difficult to seat a jury because of the emotional mind-set of the public against this kind of offense. Hard to find jurors who can be unbiased."

Josh stirred to rise again but was again held back by his father.

Jack Shaughnessey noticed that action and addressed what he suspected was Josh's concern. "Let me say something here. Anyone who leaves a dependent person in danger and does not offer assistance, where the chances of dying are most likely, is guilty of murder. That would be you, Josh."

"Also, Josh," Jack Shaughnessey continued, "Stacey disagrees with you. You say the baby was not alive. She says its arms were moving and both of you looked at each other in acknowledgement of the baby's crying, a few seconds after it emerged. We would have a difficult time at trial maintaining you did not know the baby was alive."

Josh looked down at the table.

Stacey's father, Marvin, asked Stacey's attorney, "Can you give us some specifics here, Mark? What are we talking about if they plead, or if only Stacey pleads?"

"First of all, she's being accused of Murder One alleging premeditation which apparently there was. Second, she will have a negotiable position, be able to ask for leniency because of her age and circumstance. Nothing says that leniency will be granted, but by pleading guilty and not going to trial, she has that possibility. However we should all consider the possibility of a lesser charge because once there is a plea for a First Degree Murder, that cannot be changed to a lesser sentence.

"The prosecution," Mark continued, "goes for the maximum penalty that can be supported by the evidence. What do you think, Jack?"

"As I have studied Stacey Hodgkin's situation, I can see the possibility of a life sentence, also with possibility of parole."

"Oh My God?" Adele cried out. She grabbed Stacey sitting next to her and pressed her face to hers. "Stacey... Stacey. What have you done?"

"This is just a discussion, Mrs. Hodgkins. Nothing's been decided," Mark Collins explained. Adele's husband, Marv, tried putting his arm around his wife who was tangled with Stacey. Adele was soon persuaded to release her hold on her daughter.

Mark brought the conversation back to the question of how the two defendants were going to plead - either guilty or not guilty. If it were the latter it would be that they were willing to go to trial and take their chances which were not good.

"I don't think I could live through a trial," Adele said.

Josh's father, Charlie, in his loud voice said, "I don't want my son to give up his life for something he didn't do. He says he didn't kill anybody, I believe him. I think he should stand on his innocence."

"But, Dad," Josh addressed his father, "did you hear what Mr. Collins explained. Even if I didn't kill the baby, I left it...sounds like my standing on my innocence might... be a killer..." For the first time he looked at Stacey trying to make eye-contact, but she only looked at her mother's hand on her knee.

"Son, if you go to trial and get convicted you'll be known as a killer wherever you go," his father told him.

"Dad. I won't be going anywhere."

Stacey pulled herself away from her mother's closeness. "I want to plead... guilty."

"Oh my God," Adele cried.

"I want to plead guilty." She wiped her eyes on her sleeve. "What do I do? Do I sign something?" She ignored Adele's pleading.

"No," Mark answered. " Let's hope for a good plea offer from the prosecution. You appear in court at our next court date which is five weeks from today. Unless you've changed your mind, you will be sentenced at a later date and sent to a women's state penitentiary that The Department of Corrections will select. "

Before Charlie Stockman could hold his son from standing, Josh stood up, straightened his shoulders, looked straight ahead. "I want to also," he said.

"You want to also what?" Mark Collins asked.

"I want to plead guilty."

"God Damn it son, hold off here. John," he implored John Shaughnessey, "talk some sense into Josh's head."

"Take it easy, Charlie," John Shaughnessey said. "It is Josh's decision to make. And as far as I can remember, it is the first decision different from yours he has ever made. Charlie, I'll repeat, it is *his* decision. It is *his life*. He knows what's going to happen and he's... Charlie you should be proud. He's taking responsibility for what he did."

"Hell no he's not. He just wants to be with his girlfriend."

"Charlie, he's not going to be with Stacey. They'll be in separate prisons. May not ever see each other again... ever." Josh hung his head. Stacey did not look at him. "Josh knows what he's up against. Give him credit, Charlie."

Josh's mother, Karen was quietly weeping, ignoring her husband. John Shaughnessey continued, "Your wife is not fighting her son's decision, Charlie. Let it go." He watched Josh's shoulders reverberate. "Don't make Josh more miserable than he is."

Charlie relaxed back in his chair, his mouth open, his lower lip hanging. He could say no more. He didn't bother to wipe away the tears that slowly rolled out from the corners of his eyes and down his cheek.

The attorneys organized their brief cases, stood up and shook hands agreeing to see if they could talk the prosecutors into a lesser charge than First Degree Murder.

Two sheriff's deputies entered the conference room to separately escort Josh and Stacey back to their cells, their parents jostling for a position to give their children a hurried hug, mumbling their goodbyes. Alone, they stood motionless for a moment and then walked down the grey granite stairs of the forbidding San Francisco Justice Building, into the foggy morning, hailed separate taxis, and returned to their motels.

YEARS BEFORE

ADELE AND MARV

Stacey's mother Adele, in her thinking about her daughter, was thrown back to thoughts of her own childhood, comparing her beautiful Stacey as a little girl, to herself. She was so proud of how she had raised Stacey, to give her all that she, Adele, never had, seeing Stacey as the shadow of herself as she could have been.

Adele happily worked in a dress shop in Evanston until her third child, Bobby was born, when her husband persuaded her to spend her days at home with their children.

"You've got so much to do here. Two kids in elementary to get ready for school. Sure, Stacey can get her own breakfast, but after school what does she do until you come home, to say nothing of the younger ones?"

"They do their homework. I come home only an hour after they do."

"When you first talked about a job, it was if you could be home when they all got home. I worry about them coming into an empty house," Marv told her.

"I worry too..."

"Well, it's not good. Hon, I'm making more money now, commissions are coming in. Fred is assigning more clients to me, and I'm not disappointing him."

"Marv, don't you realize how I would miss the dress shop? Nice customers, nice clothes. I get them cheaper for Stacey."

"Hon, our kids are children for such a short time. It's now they need you. As long as we can afford for you to not work, maybe you could not work until they are finished with school."

Their discussion didn't develop into another of their fights but it was an off-again-on-again sore point in their conversations for many more months. When spring ended and a long summer loomed, Adele surprised her family when she announced that she had decided to quit work at the dress shop.

"Honey," he said, putting his arms around her, "as long as we don't need the money..."

"When Stacey goes to college in two years..."

Marv cut her short. "Maybe she will be kind to our budget and go to the local community college."

"No way," Adele said, "is Stacey going to any community college. You know her grades. Has she ever gotten anything less than an 'A' ?"

Marv recognized a lengthy argument was about to start, so he didn't say what he was about to. Instead "She's one smart girl, Hon. Lots she owes you for keeping her at her books."

Reluctantly Adele became a full-time housewife, wishing she could enjoy her nice home more than she did. When she was growing up in South Chicago she always believed someday she'd have a prestigious home, landscaped with well-trimmed shrubs and multiple flower beds as she now had. She knew then she would always be happy. But it didn't turn out that way. It even seemed the more she acquired for her home or her wardrobe, the more she needed things. She replaced her Honda Civic with a Mercedes Benz, her stainless steel silverware with Oneida.

She hired a tutor for Stacey when her fear that Stacey might get a "B" in advanced placement algebra and spoil her chances of getting into an Ivy League University.

The more money Marv made, the more Adele spent to soften the hard edges of her life, the constant undercurrent reminding her she'd never be a college graduate and consequently never be a socialite, never be much of anything. In one or more of her depressions she consoled herself by reinforcing her determination that Stacey would make up for her own mediocrity.

Adele had tried so hard to make her mother proud of her, but she just couldn't get good grades, even when she copied from other's papers. Her mother paid for piano lessons for Adele, as many mothers did in those days, but Adele's efforts were pathetic.

But one thing that did please her mother was Adele's natural beauty, which tended to make up for inadequacies in school. Her good looks did not go unnoticed by the junior and senior boys. One in particular walked home with her from school several times a week. He eventually had the courage to ask her to go to the Saturday afternoon matinee, and was happy when she accepted his invitation.

Though he was three grades ahead of her, Adele and Marv became a couple. When he left Evanston to go to college in Lawrence, Kansas, Adele was heartbroken. They had a final night together before he left for his first semester. The date included a hamburger and a chocolate milkshake at the Drive-in, then a two-hour parking in the wooded local park, where both lost their virginity.

Adele cried, not knowing why.

Marv apologized, not knowing why. He hadn't forced anything: she was as transported as he was. The return to the moment was a shock.

"What if I get pregnant," she wept. "My mother... oh My God!"

"You won't get pregnant. I think you have to do it often before you can get pregnant." They hugged and kissed, and then as their emotions were about to carry them away again, they resisted the rising temptation, straightened their clothes and got ready to drive away from the area to park in front of Adele's house.

"I'm going to miss you," he said, kissing her on her forehead.

"Will you write me? Phone me?"

"You bet I will."

The first letter Marv wrote from his dormitory room was a list of all the things he had to do to register for his classes, to sign up for his room, and there was a bit about his two roommates.

Adele read the letter quickly looking for words of endearment. She read it again, but all she could find was an ending, "I miss you. Write soon."

She waited to write, being unsure of what she suspected. It was two weeks before she wrote Marv and then with a tremulous hand told him she thought she might be pregnant. She wrote that she didn't want to worry him since he was just starting college, but she thought he would want to know. She said she felt terribly guilty and was scared to tell her parents.

Marv wrote a letter to her immediately. "Honey, it's probably just a false alarm. One of the guys in the fraternity that is trying to pledge me said when girls start to have sex their hormones get all mixed up and their schedule for menstruation gets changed. Don't worry. It will be all right. Give it time. Miss you.

Day by day Adele's hope that she was not pregnant diminished. Her mother's questioning Adele's moodiness brought only more silence. Unexpectedly Marv returned from college, phoned Adele, who met him in the park. She cried when she saw him.

"Any change?" he asked as he put his arm around her. When she shook her head he asked her, "What do you want to do? I came home so we could work this out. I'll go back Monday. I can try to find a doctor who can help us."

She pulled away from him quickly, "No. I can't have an abortion. I am Catholic. And besides my mother must not know I had sex. I promised her. I swore on the Bible I would not have sex before I got married."

Marv was quiet for some time, rubbing Adele's shoulder, worried about what he was going to say. Then, firmly, "You will see a doctor. If he confirms you're pregnant, we will get married."

"I can't see a doctor. They'll report to my parents."

"We'll find... I'll find someone."

"We can't do this," Adele said. " You're in college. We'll be poor." She cried on his shoulder.

"Hon, we'll do this. I don't need to go to college. I'll get a job. We'll be okay."

"But you're marrying me just because I'm pregnant."

"Do you want your baby to have a father? I'm your man, Hon."

Adele shuddered. "Will you come with me while I tell my parents?"

"After we go together to get a doctor's opinion."

After learning that Adele was indeed pregnant, the next ordeal was to meet with Adele's mother and father. It was the worst scene the four people had ever lived through, but it put the wheels in motion, the next move being to repeat the scene with Marv's parents.

After tears and scoldings, and anger from each parent, there were eventual hugs, legal and medical details to consider, and a date to set.

Adele approached her wedding date as one going to a funeral; Marv approached the date as one unenthusiastically changing his life from a course that had been arranged his whole life, to a course unknown.

Wearing a shirt and tie and a three-piece navy blue suit he walked Chicago's business district for two days, approaching personnel managers asking for any job. He was hired as an assistant mail sorter for Goldman Sachs at the end of the second day.

He greeted Adele at her home to tell her his news as she exchanged hers, which was that she had paid one month's rent on a one-room apartment over a garage in her neighborhood for sixty-five dollars a month.

"Good," he smiled to Adele. "My pay will cover the rent, and my lunch, and our food."

"Maybe I can find a job until..."

"We'll see, Hon. Don't worry. I start my job tomorrow."

In spite of the stringent economic circumstances, their marriage was not joyless. Marv never complained that he had to drop out of college. It was a challenge for him to have a full-time job in the biggest multibanking company in Chicago.

While his job was only that of delivering mail throughout their huge building, the sheer size of the business made Marv feel important to the company, though he was only nineteen years old.

He was one of three young men who worked the large mail room, each in turn over the years promoted to assistant to a middle manager, and eventually after many years becoming middle managers themselves, acquiring accounts and earning increased commissions on hedge fund sales.

PART TWO

THE PUNISHMENT

The day of their next court appearance, *The San Francisco Chronicle's* front page headlined, *BABY KILLERS TO PLEAD GUILTY IN COURT TODAY,* which ensured a large spectator crowd. Adele attempted to remain in bed and not watch Stacey's plea proceedings. "I can't bear it. You know how nervous I get."

"Stacey needs to see you," her husband insisted. "Get up. She's got to see you." He turned to the window and shook his head, his shoulders trembling.

The court proceedings were as they had been explained to Josh and Stacey, who were brought before the court separately, with their attorney at their side. After having been read their charging documents and answering "Guilty," to each charge, they were additionally asked specifics about their guilty plea.

The questions to each were identical, to which they answered, "Yes."

"Do you understand the state's charge against you?"

"Do you waive your rights to a jury trial which gives you the privilege against self-incrimination?"

When the judge advised the court that sentencing would be in five weeks, there was a barely audible groan from the spectators who had come to hear of a closure on a story they had followed from the time they first heard of two over-privileged Stanford students disposing of an inconvenient baby.

Five months later in that San Francisco court, the bailiff once again called the case, asked the spectators to rise, and announced the arrival of judge Woodward.

"Would counselors please bring the defendants to the bench," the judge asked, and then proceeded.

"Stacey Hodgkins, for the murder of John Doe, on July 14, 2002, to which you pleaded guilty, you are charged in the Amended information as the prosecutor has changed the charge from First to Second degree murder for each defendant."

This same information was given to Joshua Stockman, with the added information, "sentencing will be in five weeks."

After that interminable five weeks, Josh, Stacy, their attorneys and their parents were back in court to hear, "Stacey Hodgkins and Joshua Stockman are hereby sentenced to fifteen years to life in state prison with the possibility of parole, but no parole hearing will be held until the fifteen years have been served. The state prisons will be determined by the Department of Corrections."

Each defendant in turn was asked by the court if they waived their rights to a trial, the right to confront and cross-examine witnesses against them, the right to testify. The defendants each answered to each question, that they waived their rights.

Then they were asked how they pleaded to Second-degree murder, to which they each answered, "Guilty, Your Honor."

Josh and Stacey were led out of the court room as the four parents tried to get near them until persuaded to stay where they were. Stacey, in spite of the sheriff deputy's restraints, inched her way toward Josh, caught his eye which she held for a brief moment with the urgency of lovers who were frightened it would be the last time.

The four parents stared at the doors closed against them and cried openly. There was no sympathy for them among the lingering spectators.

As the crowd merged together out the door and down the marble steps, the parents followed out into the chill of the San Francisco fog.

The couples took separate cabs to their separate motels on Fisherman's Wharf, packed their suitcases haphazardly and taxied separately south to the San Francisco International Airport. Between the four, no words were spoken when they saw each other fleetingly at the airport, nor did they acknowledge a goodbye nod between them.

MARV AND ADELE

After their long, cross-country flight, and their silent ride to their house in Evanston, Illinois, Marv and Adele, rather than relief that they were home, sensed that their house seemed to mock them as they entered their front door. They looked at their carefully chosen furniture, colorful drapes, accessories, even happy family pictures, but nothing gave them pleasure.

Adele who had considered herself somewhat of an interior designer, scoffed at what had once given her pride.

Neighbors of many years, friends, bridge players, who were always welcome as part of the jovial Marv and Adele Friday night dinner bridge group, now seemed shallow with their "So sorry, and time will heal." How could they be so sure?

Marv, who usually greeted his friends with a personal question to draw them to him, barely seemed even to see them, though he was better at his approach to old friends than Adele. All Adele thought about as the days went on, was surprisingly, not Stacey left behind in prison, but her thirteen-year-old daughter, Maggie.

Marv tried unsuccessfully to discourage Adele's new indulgence with Maggie. "Don't set her on those rounds of beauty pageants. Remember, sweetheart, Maggie is not Stacey. Maggie is a tomboy."

"She's a beautiful girl and will do very well, if only I can get her to see herself as a girl."

"Let her be. She's happy the way she is. Loves nothing more than pitching baseball or shooting baskets. She could care less about being a beauty queen." But Marv's attempts at persuasion were futile. Maggie's sympathy for her mother led her to go along with her mother's insistence. Maybe it would bring Adele out of her depression. The anti-depressive pills didn't do any good, but Marv soon realized it was because she was not taking them.

In the gloomy house, Marv saw their twelve-year-old Bobby as the only bright spot. For a long time Bobby refused to believe his older sister wasn't coming home. She had always been away so much at Stanford, or out somewhere with her boyfriend, Josh, so he didn't miss her much.

Bobby was the connection to the neighborhood that kept some continuity to what their family had been before his parents came back from San Francisco and said that Stacey would not be coming home for many years. He would never forget how his mother cried when his father told Maggie and him that bad news.

He remembered how his father even held his mother for a long time. Then abruptly pulled away from her and said they "needed to help Maggie and Bobby. We cannot let this spoil their lives."

Bobby saw his father kiss his mother in a way he had not done before, it had always been a kiss on the cheek as he dashed somewhere. Not this time. But it was not a happy kiss. It made Bobby so sad he had to turn away.

Things didn't seem much different to Bobby, except that his mother was always buying new clothes for Maggie. Not that he wanted any new clothes. New clothes were always uncomfortable until they were washed, when the washing took the stiffness out of them, especially the shirts.

Bobby saw that Maggie didn't care much one way or the other except their mother wouldn't let Maggie play baseball or anything in her new dresses. Besides all the girls he knew wore long pants so they could use the swings and the bars and not have to worry about showing their underpants.

"She's not as smart at Stacey," Adele complained to her husband one night when their children had gone to bed and couldn't hear her. "I don't think she can make Stanford."

"For God's sake honey, get off that track. She's only thirteen years old."

"Marv, when do you think parents start gearing their children for college, especially an Ivy League college? Going to college has to be their primary goal."

"I don't agree, Adele. Their primary goal should be to enjoy their childhood. Sure, keep up with school, but play the games. Let's not always push, push, push. Childhood is so short. Let her enjoy it."

"You should push more, Marv. Why am I the only one who always scolds when grades are not tops? "

Marv put down the evening paper he was trying to read. "Honey," he said, over -emphasizing his patience, "whose grades are they?"

"What do you mean? They are Maggie's."

"Are you sure?

"What are you insinuating?"

"What do you think? Why is it Maggie you are always barking at for better grades? What about Bobby?"

"He's still young. Maggie's in middle school. Those grades go on a transcript."

Again with excess patience Marv tried, "Adele, please back off of Maggie. She's a good kid. She's not thinking of grades for college..."

"Well she should. I'm going to bed. I don't like your criticism..."

Marv gave up, at least for this time. He'd try another time to...well he didn't know exactly. Maybe the stress and agony Adele was going through about Stacey was taking its toll on Maggie as well as on him.

Bobby, he told himself in relief, seemed to be faring okay.

It would be Marv's role to "steady the ship."

Yet he had never felt so clearly that he had to compartmentalize his life so he could deal with it. "Before," which was the only word he used to describe life before Stacey's prison sentence, he felt all the parts of his life blended together. Now there was Adele and her melancholy, her agitated pushing Maggie into beauty pageants, tutoring sessions for beginning algebra, shopping for *avant garde* clothes for young teens, all of which Maggie cared nothing about, but good-naturedly went along so as not to send Adele into a tirade that everything Maggie did would count toward her getting admitted to Stanford. Yes, it was always Stanford.

Marv would go over and over these heavy discussions with Adele. What could he say to help? Frequently torn between helping Adele and helping Maggie, he often wanted to openly take Maggie's side, if Maggie even had a side.

Maggie was such an easy-going girl. Seemed she only wanted to make others happy. If her mother wanted her to do those beauty pageants, well, okay, She'd rather be at the Saturday baseball block games, but her mother would get morose and to prevent that, it was something she'd sacrifice baseball for.

Marv's boss happened upon him when he unexpectedly brought charts to Marv's office, and found Marv staring out the window, his feet up on the sill. He had not heard Fred come in.

"Ahem," Fred cleared his throat to jokingly get Marv's attention. Marv did not turn around. "Ahem," Fred said and Marv looked over his shoulder, stood up, embarrassed.

"Sorry."

"No problem. I have these Sorenson charts. Thought it best I bring them over rather than send them through office routing." He saw that Marv was not listening, which was strange, since the Sorenson account was one of Marv's biggest.

"You okay? I know you have to go through a lot. A terrible tragedy, Marv."

"It's hard to reckon with." Marv tried to explain. "My heart goes out to Stacey and what she must be going through, and then...Oh God, I'm sorry Fred," he apologized for the tears that came unexpectantly.

Fred didn't know what to do. "Nothing to apologize for, Marv. I'll leave you alone. I'll leave these papers. We can talk about them later." Marv was embarrassed at Fred's embarrassment.

He would have to control himself, not let his personal anguish overpower his work. More than ever he needed his job to keep himself steady. His job was the only thing these days not related to what Stacey did and how it was affecting Adele and the kids. He absolutely must get back to concentrating on these Sorenson papers.

Marv realized Fred was very kind and had certainly been patient with the time off Marv had taken to console his family these last few months. But Fred's patience would not extend to losing company accounts. Marv gave himself a pep talk, trying to convince himself how he would get back to work. He'd take those charts home tonight.

And he did. Studied them on the commuter train and was ready to summarize his analysis to Fred in the morning except the evening after dinner was taken up with Adele's conversation about Maggie's tutorial with her math tutor.

"I don't think he's very good, Marv. I wish you'd kind of supervise that tutoring session, take over a bit with Maggie's algebra. Her tutor..."

"That kid with the tattoos?"

"Yes. So what. He came well recommended. Maggie likes those tattoos, kind of relates to him and that helps a bit with her accepting his advice."

"What's with advice? He either teaches or he doesn't. I don't care if he's cross-eyed as long as he's doing what we're paying him for. What are we paying him anyway?" The dinner conversation was getting heavy and Marv was happy Maggie and Bobby had finished early and been excused.

"Thirty an hour."

"What, for that kid? Why are we paying a tutor anyway? Maggie's got a math teacher at school."

"Of course she has. But she needs to get ahead of the class, and..."

"Why? Let her learn at the rate her class learns."

"Not if she wants to get those super grades."

Marv held back saying what he wanted to say, and instead, with extreme patience asked, "If *who* wants to get super grades? Adele, Maggie's only thirteen. You're going to make a basket case out of her if you don't back off."

"Marv, you better watch your blood pressure. Relax. Maggie is doing just fine. And besides she likes her tutor. That was half the battle with Stacy. I couldn't find one she liked. She argued with him, always wanted to know 'why this and that.' But she did get all A's right through trigonometry. Never would have if...hadn't..." her voice dropped to barely a hum and then the sobs came as they usually did when a conversation got too close to the edge.

Marv rounded the table, lifted Adele to a standing position and circled her in his arms. "I'm sorry, Hon, you're doing just fine whatever you're doing. We're going to be all right." But he wondered about that.

It was a cycle they went through periodically with Marv trying to get Adele to temper her desire for Maggie to be outstanding in everything she did. Bobby, on the other hand gained more freedom as Maggie lost hers.

Then as Marv tried to get Adele interested in something other than Maggie's success, he also tried to get himself to attend to his job, to be aggressive about getting more accounts to drive up his bonus points he counted on accumulating for more money at the end of the year.

He was actually complimenting himself on his focus when Fred came into his office one morning to tell Marv he had transferred the Sorenson account to David Schmidt. Marv was struck silent.

David was a young Princeton graduate in economics, hired first as an intern to learn the hedge fund dynamics. He was put on regular salary getting two important clients from the Chief Financial Officer.

Marv had watched all of David's maneuverings for position, but never thought it would personally affect him who had been with his company for twenty years and felt the security those years gave him.

To have the Sorenson account taken from him was frightening, but that it should go to David Schmidt, was humiliating. My God, he wondered, who would get those bonus points now? What Marv didn't know was that it was not bonus points he should be worried about, but his job itself.

"I'm sorry, Fred," he muttered. "I'm trying to work myself out of the way I feel about what happened to my family. It seems Stacey's tragedy has captured each of us in its web."

As he thought about what he was saying, once again he succumbed to tears.

"Marv, I don't blame you for your lack of concentration, but it is what makes our company. Focus is everything, and timing to know when to make a bid, or pull out. I have to think of the corporation. My back's to the wall too."

Marv wiped his tears with a large handkerchief he kept handy. "I am sorry, Fred. I've let you down. I'm going to..."

"Marv relax. We'll settle on a no stress marketing analysis position for you with a regular monthly salary so you don't have to worry about making bonus points. You won't make as much money, but Marv let me set up this job for you."

"I don't want charity, Fred."

"It's not charity. We need this position. I've thought about it for a long time. You'll be good. Sorry it's a come-down in pay, but we won't pressure you. Just give us a thorough analysis at the end of each month."

Recognizing how bad it could have been, that he could have been fired, Marv thanked Fred who had indeed worked for Marv's benefit. Fred walked out of Marv's office, relieved but unhappy.

What to tell Adele, he wondered. Hard for him to see her face each evening when he came home, even when he didn't have bad news. He decided he wouldn't tell her right away about his demotion.

He walked into his house and was happily greeted by Bobby who was always genuinely happy to see his father. It made the day worthwhile. What a delight at the end of a terrible day to have such a greeting.

It was Maggie he had to worry about. Could she escape the effect? Had Stacey not gotten into that trouble that she couldn't find a way out of, Adele would not be expecting Maggie to take Stacey's place as Marv saw was happening.

Somehow, he promised himself, he'd find the right course so he could help Maggie be herself.

PART THREE

THE FALL OUT

The San Francisco morning fog had not yet lifted when the prison van pulled out of the County Garage with only one prisoner — a twenty-one-year-old woman, shackled-hands and feet, hands cuffed together and attached to a waist band. She was sobbing. The van made a few sharp turns and within ten minutes was far away from the court house, bound for the two and a half hour ride to the Central California Women's Facility in Chowchilla.

The young prisoner had no interest in looking out through the barred windows at the scenery on highway, 101, the International Airport, or Highway 101 past San Mateo and Burlingame. As the van turned east, onto a connecting state road Avenue 22, Stacey began to take some interest, wanting to see what the prison would look like from the outside, a view she would not see again for fifteen years.

Her sobs that had withered to whimpers became full-blown sobs again, interrupted by blurred words, said only to herself, "I want to die... I want to die. Fifteen years? Mom, you always said, 'Things would be all right.'

How can this be all right?"

The wheels of the van crossing a patch of gravel near the entrance to the prison brought her from her slumped position. She read the signs and turned from them when the van came to a complete stop and two uniformed women came up the stairs of the van, greeted the driver and walked to Stacey's seat, indicating for her to follow them. As they neared the building one of the women removed Stacey's handcuffs.

Inside the huge, grey building she was led to a room marked "Admitting." There a large, disinterested woman wearing a name-tag with "Intake Deputy," was waiting for her. She made a hand gesture for Stacey to sit down in a chair opposite her. The seated deputy organized a few papers and then repeated the same process as had been done when she had been admitted to the San Francisco County Jail. Stacey, numb for many reasons, had difficulty focusing.

"Come with me," the deputy ordered, as they began walking through the many corridors, unlocking and locking doors, until they ascended metal stairs to the second floor and to cell number 616. She was told her bunk was the bottom one. "Your cell mate is named Myra. They are all out for recreation but will be back in twenty minutes." She walked out of the cell and locked the gate behind her

Stacey sat on the bed, rolled over to lie down, pulled her feet up to her body and whimpered, "Mom, Mom, I am so sorry." She fell into a sound sleep.

Hearing the noise of inmates returning to their cells, she fought her way out of her sleep. Her gate opened and then clanged shut, bringing Stacey to a sitting position. The woman she saw standing over her said, "I'm Myra." Myra climbed up to the top bunk. Nothing was said for awhile. Then, "It's so stinking hot out in that sun, trying to play baseball. Can't take a shower until 6:30 tomorrow morning. You've probably discovered the toilet and basin behind that half-wall there. They don't give us any privacy. There's no such thing here."

Stacey listened, not having anything to say. "The only thing," Myra continued, "the only thing private here are your thoughts. What are you in for, honey?"

"I... had a baby... and my boyfriend... well, he got rid of it." There it was. The first time she had said it.

"Wow!" Myra rolled off her bunk and stood up to hover over Stacey. "You gonna' need a ton of protection to stay alive."

"What?"

"Baby killers get knocked off pretty fast around here."

"Killed?"

"Yeah. Or wish they had been."

"Then I won't tell anybody."

"Honey, they all know all about you. I just asked you what you are in for to see if you'd tell me. Listen Honey, the only way you gonna' stay alive here is to join a 'family' for protection. You lucky you got in my 'family' for protection. I'm the Mama of family called 'Sunshine.' We got a Daddy, brothers, uncles, aunts, sisters. We all White. Races don't mix. Never."

"Let me tell you somethin' very important," Myra continued, "Don't ever make eye-contact with another race. That's an invitation to conflict. Listen, we gonna' hear the bell for lunch. The guards come by, after the master control opens all our doors at once. We get marched down to the dining room. No talking. Keep your eyes down. At the table, just look at your plate. Everybody will be looking at you. Now they leave you alone 'cause they'll know you're my new wife."

"Your wife?"

"Yeah. I have a few here. We have sex and that means no one else touches you."

"I'm not having sex with you. I don't even know how to..."

"You'll learn. We all learn if we want to stay alive. Don't worry. It's nothing romantic. We call it, 'Gay for the Stay.'"

"How can you have brothers, uncles in a women's prison?"

"We all women. We play roles. Make a family."

Josh's introduction was different, though the booking was the same. It was a long ride from the San Francisco Court House and jail, to The Richard J. Donovan Correctional Facility, on the outskirts of San Diego, near the Mexican border. He embarrassedly knew he was riding in the dark green bus with bars on the windows, clearly marked with large, white letters that it was transporting prisoners. He was the only Caucasian on the bus of about twenty-five, soon to be inmates of the Correctional Facility, all shackled, hands cuffed, and like Stacey, hands held to a band around their waist.

It had been a twelve-hour, uncomfortable ride with one stop at a MacDonalds. There the prisoners were given permission to use the lavatory, taken two at a time by one deputy. Handcuffs were removed, but ankles were still shackled. When they returned to the bus they were each given a hamburger and chocolate milkshake.

Josh slept a good part of the last leg of the trip until the increasingly loud Spanish talk wakened him. He didn't need a sign to tell him where he was. Every inch of the prison compound was lit, with a revolving search light making a continuous round of the entire prison acreage free of shrubbery where inmates might otherwise hide before trying to make a leap to freedom. Josh had no curiosity about which of the numerous buildings would be his. He had yet to accept the reality of his situation.

After the paper-work of the booking, the finger printing, the picture-taking, he was handed a stack of clothes, two sheets, one blanket, a roll of toilet paper and a bar of soap, all difficult to handle with cuffed hands.

He was led by a guard on a long walk to his cell on the third floor of a wrap-around line of cells with a cat-walk that guards paraded enabling them to look down to the large central room.

As he entered into the cell that was to be his room, he noted a man lying on the lower bunk, reading a magazine which he put to his side when the guard had opened the cell gate.

"Arnie, this is Josh," the guard announced. The two young men nodded to each other unsmiling. The guard removed Josh's handcuffs as they then both threw the clothes and linen to the top bunk. Josh climbed up to his bunk, crawled in among his things and shortly fell asleep. He was awakened hours later by the breakfast whistle and the sudden glaring light in the whole building.

As he dressed for the first time in his prison garb he asked his cell mate if they were assigned seats in the dining room.

"Of course. That's how they take roll. They take roll all day. You will soon be assigned a work station, maybe in the auto shop, or laundry, or library...there, any and all places, they do a check every three hours.

After being marched to the dining room, sitting across from a heavy-set blonde man, tatooed wherever there was skin showing, Josh was asked what he was in for.

Josh pretended not to hear. Arnie, his cell-mate nudged him and gave him a hard, brow-wrinkled stare. Josh stumbled as he spoke. "They said I was a conspirator in a murder."

"Who?"

Josh tried not to answer, but the stares penetrated his silence.

"A newborn."

"Yours?" Josh nodded.

"Better get yourself a bitch quick," one said.

Back in their cell, Arnie explained to Josh what the others meant was that he needed protection "You will only survive, "he said, "if you join a gang."

"I'm not going to join any gang. I'll take care of myself," Josh declared. "I didn't fight my conviction. I'm just here to serve my time.

"Suit yourself."

At lunch nobody looked at Josh which he welcomed. And after the evening meal he was glad to be ignored again. At nine o'clock, inmates in turn by cell block were marched to the shower room, naked except for a towel around their waist. Talking was not allowed. The only noise was the water coming from the showers, which was briefly turned off at fifteen minute intervals for the next group of men to line up under the showers when the water came back on, three men at a time under each shower head

Josh was in the last group of the day to use the showers. When it was his turn he stood under the shower waiting for the water to come on when he noticed one of the men next to him was his celly. He was about to acknowledge him when his celly grabbed him, twisted one arm behind his back, pushing his face into the wall while the third man began to rape him. As Josh yelled for help, his celly rammed a knife or something into his side. Two guards rushed to them, separated the three and took the two attackers away. Josh slumped to the floor and noticed blood flowing toward the shower drain. One hand brushed an object on the floor he saw as a toothbrush. Perplexed he picked it up without anyone noticing, quickly stood up, grabbed his towel off the hook, secreting the toothbrush in the edge of the towel which he wrapped around himself as he exited the shower and joined the men marching back to their cells. He was aware of blood running down his legs but pretended not to notice. One man mumbled something to another so the guards would not hear, but which Josh did. The word he caught was "shu" which he knew was slang for "Solitary Confinement Unit". That would be, he assumed, for the two men involved in his rape.

When the gate to his cell clanged behind him he realized because his 'celly' was in "shu", he was alone for the first time on his first day. He sat on his bed, examined the toothbrush, studied the bit of razor attached to the end which he decided must have been immeshed in the plastic end of the toothbrush handle after it had been heated someway and was pliable. He wiggled the piece of razor but it was as if he didn't.

He lay down on his bed, drew the razor end of the toothbrush under his chin from ear to ear and felt the blood spurt. It was the last thing he felt.

CHARLIE, KAREN, MARV

Josh's father, Charlie, woke up in his bed in Evanston, Illinois, a few hours after Josh was found dead in the California prison which had yet to contact Josh's parents. Charlie was looking for something, his eyes moving from walls to window, his breathing coming faster. He reached over and nudged his sleeping wife.

"Karen. Wake up. I just realized something."

"For Pete's sake, Charlie, go back to sleep. It's barely light outside."

"Karen, listen, listen..."

"I don't hear anything. Go back to sleep."

"I can't sleep. I just realized... I'm a grandfather."

"You're a what?"

"A grandfather."

Karen half-way sat up. "Don't do this, honey. Don't do this. Don't even think about it."

"We can go fishing."

"Charlie..."

"Remember when I took Josh fishing. He loved it. Loved putting those worms on the hook."

Karen looked sympathetically at her husband, but decided sympathy would not help him. She explained that Josh hated fishing. "He only went with you because you wanted him to. He hated putting those squirming worms on the hooks while they were still alive."

Charlie did not hear her. "He loved fishing. I can see him now." Thoughtful for awhile, he then asked,

"Did they give him a name?"

"What do you mean? Oh... no, honey. Give it a rest. This will drive you crazy..."

"I'm going to give him a name. I'm going to call him Duggan. Yes, Duggan."

"Charlie, please," she begged.

"So I can call him 'Duggie'." He rolled over on his side. "That's it, yes, Duggie."

"Charlie", Karen pleaded, softly crying. "Don't make it worse than it is."

"Worse? No," he pulled the covers up over his huge shoulders. "Worse? No. I'm going to make it better. Hon the phone's ringing. Will you get it."

Karen turned over to face her nightstand and picked up the phone's receiver. "Hello. Yes. What bad news. Is Josh sick? What did you say? Who is this? The Warden? Are you sure you have the right number? Yes, this is Karen Stockman. His birth date? It is September 9, 1982. Middle name? Arnold."

Karen dropped the receiver to the floor, fell back on the bell and bellowed with weeping. "He's dead." She turned to move next to her husband for consoling. He was the strong one. He looked at her not knowing her.

"Charlie, Josh is dead. He died in the sick room. Got sick or something. Charlie," she clutched him, "He got sick, must have been on that bus ride. He got sick. Now,... Stacey is alive... Josh is dead... our boy!" She clung to Charlie, frantic in her misery.

Charlie put his arm around Karen's shoulder, confused, wondering who the lady hanging on to him was. The phone rang.

"Get the phone, Hon," Charlie said, pushing Karen aside.

Automatically Karen rolled across the bed and picked up the receiver. "Is that you, Charlie?" the man's voice said.

"No. This is Karen. Who is this?"

"Karen, this is Marv Hodgkins. I just learned there will be a news article in the obituaries in the *Evanston Star* this morning about Josh's... death. One of the reporters called me, wanted to verify that this was one of our star football players a couple of years ago. I told him, sadly it was. I just wanted to give you a head's up to try to prepare you. Terrible news. No, I don't have any information. I'm offering my sympathy. Anything I can...

Karen put the receiver back on the phone and shoved the phone until it fell onto the floor where she could still hear Marv's voice as she lay back on the bed, stupefied.

Because there was no closure on the telephone, Marv sensed he should drive the few blocks to Karen and Charlie's house. When he did, Karen opened the door in her bathrobe, her hair tangled, her eyes red with crying.

"I am so sorry, Karen," Marv said as Karen held the door open for him. Even though the two families had never been on friendly terms, Marv had a strong impulse to take her in his arms and console her. But he refrained.

"I am so sorry I blurted out about Josh over the phone. I didn't know what to do."

"Don't worry about that. I knew about it just before your call. The warden phoned me. Come into the kitchen. I have coffee."

Settled around the kitchen table in silence, Karen and Marv sat staring at their coffee cups, when Charlie shuffled in, in his bathrobe and slippers. Marv stepped forward to give Charlie a hand shake, but Charlie stepped back, frowning.

"He doesn't recognize you," Karen told Marv under her breath. "Only occasionally recognizes me." She continued staring at her coffee cup. "I want to go out to California," she said. "See what happened. Don't know what to do with Charlie."

Marv pondered and then offered, "Let me call your doctor. Get you some help."

"Whatever," Karen answered.

Ten days later, Marv drove Karen to the Westmore Funeral Home in Evanston where Josh's body had been shipped from San Diego with the help of Marv's arrangements with the prison. He asked Karen if she wished him to go into the building with him.

"Yes, please, but wait in the lobby."

A half hour later she came out of the private viewing room, red-eyed but silent. At her house, Marv helped her out of his car and told Karen, "Call me anytime."

STACEY

Marv made periodic phone calls to Stacey's attorney, Mark Collins, wanting to know about prison visiting times, but was frustrated when the news from Mark indicated Stacey should not have visitors for at least two months. The weeks dragged on with Adele nearly frantic with worry about her daughter. Was she eating? Was she being raped by other women, or by the guards? She'd heard that happened in prisons. She had to know what was going on. She was Stacey's mother. She had a right to know.

Marv fielded her questions as best he could, caught between wanting to sooth Adele's anxieties, yet giving her enough information to let her know it would be a long wait to see Stacey.

"Why can't we just go see her? She's our child."

"Well, in a way she's not anymore, Honey. She belongs to the State. We have to accept..."

"We don't have to accept that we can't see our own child. It's enough she's taken from us, but at least we should be able to visit her."

It was the same conversation each week, and it always ended in tears with Marv consoling Adele.

"Honey," Marv would remind her, "we have her letters. Consider them as visits until we can actually see her. And, Honey, try to be more upbeat when you write her."

"Don't tell me how to be. How can I pretend to be happy when I've never been more miserable."

Almost despairing, but wanting to make things more bearable for Stacey, Marv reminded Adele that Stacey was also miserable. "Try to make it better for her, not worse."

Then Adele would sting him. "I hate you. You have no idea how I feel. You have a job you go to everyday and I'm here getting groceries, picking the kids up at school, taking them to all the things they're involved in, looking cheerful while my heart is breaking."

"Honey, my heart is breaking too. Remember, Stacey is my daughter too." At this point Marv would leave the room, Adele sobbing but not getting comfort from her husband.

When Mark Collins did get back to Marv with good news about a visitation date for Marv and his family, Adele indicated she did not want to go.

"I look so awful. Stacey will see how much weight I have lost."

Out of patience Marv simply said, "I need to go. I need to see Stacey, whether you go with me or not. Since you don't seem to want to make the trip, that's okay. I'll take Maggie and Bobby. They need to see their sister. I'm getting visitation information for Chowchilla from Mark. Maggie's been asking about Stacey. Says maybe she's not even alive. How would she know if she doesn't see her."

"I want to see her, Marv. But not in prison. That would be too much. No... you go ahead."

Mark sent Marv a list of do's and don'ts for prison visitation, including telling Marv Chowchilla encourages family and friends to keep in regular visitation contact so inmates can more easily return to society.

It was difficult for Marv to ask his boss, Fred, for time off to fly across the country to see his daughter, but too much time had passed already.

His boss, who was usually understanding and compassionate, was not so this time. "The company has been losing money since we lost that last account. Take two days, maybe go a Friday before a weekend and return on the Monday."

"Visitation is only on weekends and holidays, so that will be fine. Thank you, Fred."

Marv did not know how he could leave Adele behind, but she would not budge on her determination. How could a mother not see her daughter? The only peace of mind he could give himself about leaving her alone, was to face the fact that Adele just had not been the same as she was before Stacey was sentenced.

He was packed with mixed feelings, worried more about what Stacey's reaction would be when she did not see her mother in the family group, than about Adele's change of personality.

Bobby and Maggie chatted the whole plane ride from Illinois to California, ignoring the games they had brought along to play on the trip. From the airport in the rental car to the motel miles from the airport, they were more interested in the rural landscape in central California than games or conversation.

They found the motel recommended by the prison's Ombudsman, checked in, threw their suitcases in their rooms, and sped on to the Visitor's Entrance of The Central California Women's Facility in Chowchilla.

They were greeted by a welcoming staff- member who checked them through the lengthy security process, and led them into the Family Visiting Center. He asked them to sit at a specific table, saying that Stacey would be joining them soon. They were told the family was permitted to hug Stacey at the beginning of the visit and again before they left in six hours. But they could return the following day, on Sunday.

At first when Stacey walked into the large, noisy room filled with family and friends of the inmates, Marv and his children couldn't talk, being so emotionally engulfed. Questions eventually were asked about why Stacey's mother wasn't there, and answered however untruthfully or sketchily.

Maggie, staring at Stacey like she didn't want to stop for fear of losing her, said, "I didn't miss you so much when you were in college. But now I just keep waiting for you to come home."

"Me too," Bobby added. "I was forgetting what you looked like, and it had only been two months. Dad had some pictures of you blown up so we could put them by our bed for us to look at when we said our prayers."

When Marv encircled Stacey in his arms, he began to cry and couldn't stop. His three children crowded over him, also crying until one of the guards separated them.

Eventually, determined to not have the visit completely sad, Marv gently broke the hold, and said to Stacey, "Tell us what you do here so when we think of you we can picture you."

Relieved to break the grip grief had on her, Stacey told them of her job in the shop and later in the kitchen, getting cereal ready for the inmates for breakfast, and being the chief salad maker at lunch and dinner.

Marv asked, "Do you sleep okay. Stacey?"

"Yes. I'm so tired because I have to study when I'm through work."

"Study? Here?" Bobby asked.

"Yes. I wrote Mom. Maybe she forgot to tell you." She turned to talk to her father. "I enrolled in an on-line program. It's in Alamosa, Colorado, but I can do my work on the tablet supplied to good-behavior inmates by this prison. I use the money I make in the dining room, seventy-five cents an hour, to pay for my units. I'll get a degree in Business Administration. Mom wouldn't like that subject, but it is something I could use when I get out of here."

"Why?" Bobby insisted. "I thought if you were in prison you'd never have to go to school again."

"I have almost two years of college at Stanford. If I can pass all my courses on line, I can get my degree."

"But why?" Bobbie asked again.

"It was one of Mom's goals for me. She never got to go to college and my going... well, I'm doing it for her. But she would want me to go for a degree in art history, or something fancy, nothing I could use."

Marv shuddered: Stacey noticed. "But I'm doing it for me, too, Dad. It's the one thing I look forward to... studying at night."

Bored by the conversation, Bobby and Maggie ran across the room to see another woman being led into the room, carrying a tiny baby. Bobbie and Maggie stood on tiptoe to see its face.

Out of her siblings' hearing, Stacey solemnly told Marv, "Dad, I know about Josh. My cellmate told me, she helped me. It was terrible to hear what he did. Ava, that girl who just came in the room with the baby, she helped too. She's my friend. She had her baby in prison and she let me hold him right after it was born."

"I didn't know they delivered babies in prison," Marv said.

"Yes. They can't keep the babies here, but it helps them on their good behavior. They have something to help them stay out of trouble, knowing they have a baby on the outside when they get out."

When Marv saw Stacey's tears, he took her hands in his and said, "Honey. I'm glad you have friends here."

"It's terribly sad for these pregnant girls. They never get visits from their boyfriends. I guess the boys feel they are well out of their trouble. I learned that eighty-five percent of inmates are mothers. And hardly anyone comes to see them. Somewhere there are their children on the outside they might find when they get out."

"When I made friends with Ava," Stacey continued, "she was five months pregnant, but her baby came prematurely. I saw her the next day just when they brought her baby into the ward. They handed the baby for Ava to hold for about fifteen minutes. Ava looked frantic. It was a sad- happy moment."

Marv suggested, "That must have been a kind of torment for you." He put his arm around Stacey's shoulders just as she burst into sobs.

"I almost couldn't stand it, Dad. I had a great impulse to grab that baby and run. For the first time I saw so clearly what I had done. How could I? What a monster!"

She went on. "I kept telling myself since all I did was give birth I was not responsible for what happened to it after that. Now, I think what a terrible thing for Josh to have to do. What determination it must have taken." She tightened her arms around her father's neck, "How I wish I could beg his forgiveness. That poor guy! I know now why I loved him. He did it for us, no matter what anyone else says. We always loved each other. He was my life."

––––––––––––––

The first visit day for Stacey's family was on the whole quite happy as they had another day to look forward to. But the second day was filled with the apprehension that they'd have to leave in the afternoon and never know when they could make the long trip again.

When the guards signaled the end of visiting hours on the second day, the four huddled tightly. "Dad," Stacey cried, "tell Mom I'm sorry. I'm sorry I'm a disappointment for her."

At those words, Marv cried openly, wanting to reassure Stacey that her mother loved her no matter what, but words would not come.

It was a room of massive sorrow as family and friends hugged each other until the last bell rang indicating one minute before the end of visiting hours. The large center was filled with loud cries as young children were pulled from their mothers and mothers tried to hold onto their children.

As for Marv and his family, the guard gently separated the three from the one, who was left standing alone until being led to the long hallway leading back to her cell. Her family walked backwards for as long as they could see her.

In her cell, Stacey lay on her bunk and wept, saying she couldn't do this. "This is worse than death. I can't do this."

After a half-hour, tears spent, she sat up, wiped her cheeks with her sheet, reached toward her bookcase and pulled down, "Diminishing Returns on Capital and Labor." The notepad inside the book indicated where she had left off studying, and that is where she began taking notes, or tried to.

Her mind turned from her text book to all the bad things of prison, the roll call five times a day, the constant sense that the guards or deputies were watching the inmates incessantly.

But mostly she resented the sense of fear she had built up. Every little rule infraction could count as a demerit and affect whether the guard said the inmate could not have visitors the following weekend, or not have laundry facilities for that week. She could even get sent to the "hole" which was solitary confinement for as long as the guard could persuade his boss the infraction warranted. Any other demerits might be enough to extend sentence time, which would be the worst thing to happen.

"Going home," Stacey realized was the inmates' primary goal. Prisoners would suffer unfair punishment rather than risk adding "time" to their stay away from their families.

Stacey felt sorry for the inmate mothers, especially vulnerable to enduring humiliation. There were a few guards or deputies who were helpful to inmates, but Stacey could see they didn't consider kindness to inmates as the primary focus of their job. While Stacey had thought most inmates would consider their sentencing as "a bum rap," that wasn't what she found. Most considered they had made a wrong choice. They wished they hadn't been caught, but did not hold themselves innocent of the charges.

Keeping order and preventing riots were paramount considerations of guards and deputies. Stacey learned from speaking to new transfers to Chowchilla that the emphasis in other prisons was similar. Free speech was out. If one wanted to simply serve their time and leave, the hardest goal for all, especially those who had been fighting "the system" all their lives, was to "hold their tongue."

Stacey saw her job as simply staying out of trouble. Don't sass a guard even if he was totally wrong. Don't complain or what she would be complaining about would be made worse for her. She saw this happen to the weakest of the women. Trying to ease a situation for another inmate was a ticket to earning demerits.

While she resented Myra, her "protector," Stacey learned to value her. She was sure she escaped worse treatment than she endured, because Myra was held in some awe by the guards. Stacey learned that Myra's gang connections outside prison indirectly benefited both Myra and Stacey and Myra's other protected inmates. Stacey also realized the guards did little to trim the power of gangs inside prison because they helped to keep order, though she never heard it discussed.

Getting a good prison job with only a few inmates to mingle with would probably be the best way to keep herself out of trouble. That job turned out to be a job in the shop. Not many women had much skill with repairing furniture by gluing sections together or getting larger screws to hold table legs to table tops, or knew how to splice electric wires to get old lamps and worn-out light electrical fixtures to function, or to unplug a stopped up sink or toilet. Mostly these were two-person jobs and not like working in the laundry where twenty or more women jabbered and argued as they folded sheets and towels. Too likely to get in a fight there.

But when more help was needed in the kitchen, Stacey was transferred there. She reminded herself to not get caught up in any confrontation.

As difficult as it was to take a day at a time, seeing the years spread out before her, she knew it was the only way she could survive. She missed Josh and dare not give herself in to thinking about him, and what drove him to take his life. If only she could have talked to him, given him some hope for a future down the line. With good behavior they could get out in eleven years considering the four years they'd spent in jail waiting trial. There could be years together. Then with those thoughts she would give into the sorrow, reflecting on things they would do together. First a few tears wet her hands as they held her face. Then came the deluge, almost impossible to stop. She'd have to quit indulging herself in those thoughts.

Reading her textbook, her mind drifted and she found herself thinking again of Myra. In spite of the circumstances of their relationship, Stacey developed a close bond with her, though constantly reminded by her protector to not count their attachment as anything more than a necessary arrangement.

"As a 'lifer' I will be here forever, and you will be gone before you know it," Myra warned Stacey, hoping to curb Stacey's emotional dependence on her, especially when Myra noticed signs of jealousy from Stacey when Myra was with her other "protectees."

The power-hierarchy was clear-cut and not to be tested by neophytes without severe penalties. Guards looked the other way as long as there was order.

One of Stacey's close friends was the young mother, Ava, of the newborn baby boy, who let Stacey hold her baby shortly after it was born. Ava had not settled on a name for her baby though she knew if her family did not come to claim it within forty-eight hours, it would be given to the Child Protective Services, nameless, where it would wait to be placed with a foster family until an adoptive family came to take it into their family.

The social worker told Ava if she didn't pick a name to put on the birth certificate, the prison would do that for her. Ava wanted to name it after the father, but since he was in prison for selling heroin, and was very ill, she was hesitant. She had no affection for the father. Ava told Stacey she also thought about naming it after her own father, but he had deserted her family when she was less than a year old. She wondered why her mother had kept a tattered picture of him on her dresser.

"I can't just name him nothin'," Ava told Stacey.

"Can I give him a name?" Stacey asked.

"What would it be?"

"Joshua. He was a man I was in love with, all my life who is now dead."

Just before handing her crying baby to Stacey who handed it to the social worker, Ava quickly wrote in the birth certificate on her lap, the name, *Joshua Arnold Jorgenson*, that last name being Ava's last name.

When Stacey held baby Josh, she had an immediate connection to the infant who seemed to smile at her in the warmth of Stacey's arms.

MARV AND ADELE

Back in Evanston, the day after their visit with Stacey, Maggie and Bobby returned to school and their father returned to his job. Their mother Adele wanted to ask questions about her imprisoned daughter, but couldn't bring herself to ask. That for her would make the whole experience real.

At work Marv forced himself to concentrate on the tedious details of the statistical summaries of the company's history. Dreary numbers, Marv told himself, were difficult to make interesting.

He found himself longing for a talk with Josh's mother Karen, about her loss of Josh. He wondered often how she could get through the days. He wanted to console her and to hear her talk of Josh and of Josh's time with Stacey. There was even one night he woke from a dream that the baby at Stacey's prison was Josh's baby. But he shook it off knowing dreams could get mixed up with what was going on in the day time. He resisted making a phone call to Karen as long as he could, but that length of time closed in on him.

One sleepless night he silently got out of bed without disturbing Adele, crept down the stairs and sat in his office chair with the phone in his hand for over a half-hour before he put the phone back in its cradle, went back up stairs and remained sleepless next to Adele for the rest of the night.

He didn't understand himself. Adele and he had never really liked Stacey's boyfriend's parents. Weren't keen on Stacey's attachment to their son, Josh, but felt the attachment would pass. Yet why was he so drawn to Josh's mother? And why did he torture himself going over and over what had to be for Karen an almost unbearable sadness. The more he asked himself that question, the more he wanted to keep asking it.

The boring, detail recounting of the company's history made it easy for his mind to drift. It was best, he kept telling himself, that he not contact Karen, no matter how much he wanted to console her. Yet he couldn't prevent an accidental meeting. It was at Von's Supermarket as he stood waiting in the check-out line. In the line next to the one Marv was in, Karen was looking at him.

As they finished checking out their groceries, they walked together wordlessly toward their cars until Marv said, "I owe you a cup of coffee."

They stopped. Karen looked around the mall, spotted a Starbucks, nodded in that direction. They emptied their groceries in the trunks of their cars and walked together to Starbucks.

Sipping their Cafe Lattes, Marv told Karen he and his children had been to see Stacey.

"Oh, My! How is she doing? So young and in with all those tough women!"

"She's miserable, but typically she tries to project that things were okay."

"Did she know about Josh?"

"Yes. She didn't talk much about what she knew. I could cry every time I think about what she and Josh had gone through." He paused a minute, reflecting. "But nothing like what you are going through."

After a time, Karen said, "Josh couldn't take it. He always acted tough, I think to please his father, but he was really a sensitive person. He hurt for other people... hurt for himself but didn't talk about it. He knew complaining about things was a sign of weakness according to his father."

Karen continued, "What is so hard for me is that I don't know what he died of. Had he been stabbed or something?" She rummaged in her purse for a tissue.

"Maybe time will tell," Marv offered weakly.

Abruptly he changed the subject. "How's Charlie?"

Karen shook her head, dabbed at her eyes. "He's living in a board and care residence. I can't take care of him. He can't even dress himself."

"Does he..." Marv ventured "know where he is?"

"No. And he doesn't know me." She stifled a sob. "I talked to a psychiatrist about him. He told me that when real life is too difficult for the mind to accept, a person sometimes makes up his own perception of things, an alternate reality, is what he called it. It helps him to tolerate the life he has. Charlie has regular hallucinations that he is playing baseball with a little boy named Duggie. He pretends that Duggie is his grandson."

Karen could not go on. Seeing her tears brought tears from Marv who reached across the table, palm open. Karen immediately put her hand in his.

After another half hour of mostly silence, they left, walked to Karen's car where Marv put his arm around her and drew her to him. She encircled his shoulders and burst into tears.

"Compared to hell," she said, "this is heaven."

He opened the car door for her and said he would call her soon, most likely late at night. "Would that be all right?" he asked.

"That would be very nice," she answered.

MAGGIE

Maggie, fresh from having seen Stacey, decided she wasn't going to wait another month before seeing her again. Maggie didn't like some of the inmates she saw in Stacey's prison... thought they looked tough and dangerous. She wondered if maybe she could get Stacey out of there. Not much of a chance, but maybe she should try.

She looked at the small box for money she kept under her underwear in her dresser drawer, counted it out, spread it out on her bed. She had one hundred sixty-four dollars and thirty-two cents. She kissed the one-hundred dollar bill her father's mother had given her last Christmas as her first donation for Maggie's college fund. She wondered how much it would cost to fly to Chowchilla, or rather Fresno, the airport forty miles from the prison.

Good on the computer, she learned from Google the airfare would be one hundred thirty-two dollars and seventeen cents. She would worry about getting home after she got there. She would take a backpack stuffed with pajamas, an extra pair of jeans, underpants, and a sweatshirt. That should do it.

The next day when Adele drove to pick her up from the school bus, Maggie was not on the bus. She cell-phoned Maggie's school and learned she had been absent from her last period class. She phoned the Evanston police, then phoned Marv. Both he and Adele were asked many questions by the police.

"Were there any arguments before Maggie left for school this morning?"

"No."

"Did the morning seem normal?"

"Yes, didn't pay much attention," Marv said.

"Had she talked of wanting to go anywhere?"

"No. We just came back from California."

"What were you doing there?"

"Visiting her sister."

"Anything special about how she feels about her sister?"

"She adores her sister," Adele answered.

The police left the house, telling Marv and Adele they would be in touch, would alert trains, busses, and airlines to be on the lookout for a thirteen-year-old by herself, with a backpack, or any situation where a girl was with other people and looked out of place with them.

Marv didn't wait for any telephone call. As soon as the police drove off in their police car, he backed his car out of their driveway and headed for Chicago, not telling Adele where he was going, which was the O'Hare Airport.

There on a bench by the ticket sales counter he saw Maggie sitting by herself, her backpack by her side. She looked up, surprised. "Dad, what are you doing here?"

"No, Maggie. The question is, 'what are *you* doing here? You had your mom and me scared to death. Thought someone had run off with you. Christ, what a relief." He picked her up from the bench and hugged her.

"Where were you going?" He sat down beside her, holding her hand.

"Back to Stacey. Dad, I couldn't stand to see her there. I didn't want her to know how awful I thought it was, but I thought about it all the way home. I had to get her out of there, out of that awful uniform, all those big junkie women around her. I'm afraid for her, Dad."

Marv grabbed her around her shoulders and rocked her back and forth. "Honey, honey, honey."

"They wouldn't sell me a ticket, unless a parent was with me and would sign me over to a stewardess. But now you're here..."

"No, Honey. We have to go home and talk about this. This is too much for you to fix. I don't want to lose another daughter. When you do things like this, you have to think of other people you might hurt. Come on, let's go see Mom. God, how happy she will be." He took out his cell phone and made that happy call.

"Dad, how did you know where to find me?"

"I don't know. But when you know your kid, you kind of know how she thinks."

On the road back to Evanston, Maggie asked, "Dad, since Mom sleeps in the guest room now, can I sleep with you from now on?"

"No, Honey, That would be inappropriate."

"What's that mean?"

"It's not something we can do."

"I miss Stacey so much. When she came home from college she always let me sleep with her. We'd talk and then I'd turn with my back to her and she would put her arm over my shoulder and I'd feel... safe."

"Have you been scared?"

"Sure. All kids are."

"What are you afraid of?"

"Everything. That I'll wake up in the morning and everyone will be gone. What's 'inappropriate' mean?"

Marv drove on, wondering how to close this part of the conversation.

"How did you get money for an airplane ticket?"

"Grandma. She gave me money for college. Said I should hide it, not let Mom know, that she would add to it every birthday and Christmas and by the time I was ready for college I'd have enough money."

"Mmmm... I'll have to talk to grandma about that."

"So can I sleep with you? It's the only time when I am all alone. You or Mom tuck me in, turn off the light, leave the room, shut my door. It's a scary time."

"Maggie, you're a big girl now. Almost a teenager, almost a woman. A father can't sleep with a daughter who's a woman. That's what 'inappropriate' means. Why don't you see if Mom would let you sleep with her," he suggested.

"I don't want to sleep with Mom."

"Why not."

"Just don't."

Maggie's mother worried most of her day about Stacey. Maggie's father worried about Stacey and frequently about Maggie. She was labeled a "juvenile runaway" by the Evanston Police Department, but there were no charges against her. She was assigned a court appointed therapist, Alice, for Maggie to meet with if she wanted to. Maggie liked Alice, but really didn't have much to say to her. Mostly Alice would ask how things were going in school.

"Nothing special," Maggie would usually respond.

"Friends?"

"Yeah. Don't hang out with them much."

"Why not?"

"Don't have much to talk about. They're still into... Oh, I don't know... kid stuff."

"Like what?"

"Oh, they chase each other at recess, playing tag like we used to do in Grammar School. Or talk about the clothes other girls are wearing. I just take a book out to recess."

"Don't teachers tell you how important it is to get exercise?"

"They've given up on me. Mostly leave me alone. Which is good."

After a silence, Alice asked, "What are you reading?"

Maggie turned the book over in her hand. "You mean right now?"

"Right now. What's that book?"

"*Catcher in the Rye*. Do you know it?"

"Uhmmm. It was required reading in my senior English class in high school. It's a bit advanced for a thirteen-year-old."

"If I understand it, is it too old for me?" Maggie asked.

"No. I guess not." Alice paused. "How are things at home... with your mother? "

"She's backed off a little. If I go to a few things willingly, she'll not force me to everything. Even to a ladies' tea. Can you imagine me at an afternoon tea?"

"Well, maybe not at a tea, but what else?"

"Oh, she has all these beauty pageants she signs me up for. Most of them are all in other towns and on a Saturday when our baseball team plays. I try to get out of those silly dress-up shows. But if I participate in some it takes the pressure off."

"How you getting along with your dad?"

"Good. He's on my side. They fight a lot. Never did that when Stacey was home."

"Why is that, do you think?"

"I don't know. Mostly because Stacey just did what she was told. I don't think I ever heard her say she didn't want to do something. I think she kind of liked all that pageant stuff and walking around the house with a book on her head."

"Do you ever have any more urges to run away?"

"I didn't run away. I had to go see Stacey. I hate it without her. I could have taken care of her baby." Maggie's tears brought an end to that conversation.

"Do you want to go home, Maggie? Had enough for today? I think you're doing fine."

Without a word, Maggie walked out of the room in the police department and began the three mile walk home. But she wasn't through with the questioning which started again as she walked in the front door.

"What did they quiz you about today, honey," her mother asked.

"I don't know, Mom, the usual... 'Are you happy at home? Do you want to run away again? How are your friends?' I'm going to my room, got a bunch of French verbs to memorize for a test tomorrow.

"Just a minute, Maggie. When you came in did you see Bobby playing with Michael, you know, the Lopez boy?"

"I didn't see anyone."

"I'll call their house. Wonder why your father is late again." She heard Maggie's bedroom door close at the same time the front door opened and Marv entered, putting his brief case on the hall table and stepping to embrace Adele, who pulled away from him.

"Why are you so late?" Adele asked.

"I ran for the El but missed it. Long wait for the next. Sorry, Hon. Have the kids eaten yet?"

"Bobby's over at the Lopez house I think. Maggie's upstairs learning French verbs, and the roast is drying out in the oven."

"Well then, phone the Lopez boy, get Bobby home, and get Maggie down here and let's eat." He glanced at the dining room table and saw that it was not set for dinner. He figured they must be eating in the breakfast room.

Adele had noticed Marv's glancing at the dining room table and quickly offered, " I'll set the breakfast table."

"Get Maggie to do that," Marv urged.

"She needs to study until dinner is on the table. I'll do it."

Marv reached over to Adele and took her hand. "Hon," he said, " she needs to help around here. Don't try to make a Barbie Doll out of *her*."

"Marv, please. She has to get her grades up. Seems to be just dragging along. Kids don't get into Ivy League Schools with 'B's' in high school."

Marv dropped Adele's hand, looked down at the floor. "Hon, there are worse things than not getting into an Ivy League."

Adele slumped into one of the kitchen chairs, folded her hands and stared straight ahead. "You have no idea what I have been going through. I've got a second chance here with Maggie. It was easier with Stacey. She was smarter and she wanted what I had wanted for her. Maggie just goes along, but she has no enthusiasm. I have to keep reminding her about 'A's' even if she's only in Junior High or what they now call Middle School. "

Marv was about to interrupt, but Adele continued. "School is Maggie's most important job right now."

"Damn it, Hon, Maggie's still a kid. Her most important job is to be a kid, have fun with other kids, even have fights and get over them, work out getting along with her friends. Learn to make her own decisions."

Adele stood up, stared at Marv. "What are you now, a psychiatrist?" She walked out of the breakfast room, her shoulders shaking. She shot back at him, "Are you saying I lost Stacey because she couldn't make good decisions?"

Marv mumbled to the closed door. "She not only couldn't make good decisions, she couldn't make *any* decisions."

The front door opened as Bobby ran into the house, looked into the living room, then ran into the breakfast room. "Hi Dad. Did you just get home? Where's Mom? Is dinner ready?" Not waiting for any answer, he ran up the stairs, opened and then slammed his bedroom door, leaving Marv in the breakfast room, alone with his thoughts.

After a few minutes, Adele returned to set the table, turn off the oven, and at the same time turn off the boiling water which was ready for the asparagus.

"Adele, Hon, can I say something without getting into another one of our fights? Will you sit down a minute?"

Adele slowly sat, ready to listen.

Marv took her hand. "Hon, we still have two children at home. Stacey, though not home, is still very much alive and making the best of a terrible situation. So are Maggie and Bobby trying to make the best of what has happened to them. We must raise all three and not just concentrate on Maggie"

Adele frowned at Marv. "Are you accusing me of ignoring Bobby?"

"I am not accusing you of anything. I am saying we've got to help all three."

He was silent a moment and then told Adele, "I cry for Stacey." He fought back tears. "She has lost her mother who won't visit her, and she can see her father and Maggie and Bobby only once every month for two days, trips which incidentally are exhausting our savings."

"You could go more often."

"You aren't listening. I am using up our savings to make the trips as it is. I'm hanging on to my job by a thread. We're getting low on funds. I was curious if I could petition the Department of Corrections to see if we can get Stacey in a prison nearer to her home. But I didn't try because Stacey seems to think she wants to stay in Chowchilla, that her friends there have become important to her. She's afraid her academic records she's earned there will get lost if she moves and she is looking forward to getting that business degree."

Adele said nothing.

Marv continued, "I'd sell this house if it would help us. I'd live in a tent in the park if it meant the kids and I could see Stacey more often. Seems to be what keeps her going. Us, and her school, and her friends there."

Not concerned whether Adele was listening or not, he talked to himself more than to anyone else. "Poor Maggie. I heard her crying after she went to bed last night. I opened her door, saw her talking to Roscoe, her Teddy Bear. Hon, it was like she was a five-year-old, telling Roscoe how she missed Stacey and she said when she left her at the prison every time she was afraid she'd never see her again."

"I sat on the bed with her and cried, and moved up our visiting date." He looked at Adele, "Don't you think you'd like to join us this time? It would make Stacey happy."

Adele stood up. "Marv," she said, wiping away tears that would not fall, "please don't ask me again to do that. Stacey was my dream. Think what it would be to see your dream in prison. It's a nightmare."

"Adele, Hon," Marv pleaded. "If I get an appointment at the psychological clinic with their best doctor, would you go with me?"

"I don't want to go crying from doctor to doctor. No one can turn the clock back. What's done is done."

BOBBY

Bobby ran down the stairs and plopped himself in the breakfast-room chair next to his father.

"I wish you knew more about computers, Dad. I'm stuck."

"What are you trying to do?"

"I'm programming a game and can't seem to store it on my flash drive."

"I can show you how to do that."

"No. The flash drive is not accepting it. I don't want to lose what I have."

"I'll tell you what. Go on Google and ask the question you just asked me."

"Yeah, or maybe I can figure it out. I wish Stacey had a computer in prison. We could play games."

"She has a tablet. The state gives them to inmates, but they put limitations on them and there are censors who won't let information out if it is suspicious. But games maybe could be cleared. She has to post receivers' names who are then investigated."

"Me?"

"Yes. Give it a try."

"How do I get her email?"

"It's the same as it was here, but she has to get clearance."

"Dad. Have you been emailing her?"

"Yes. When I can say something cheerful."

Bobby gulped his cereal and bounded back up stairs.

"Dad," he announced a few minutes later, skipping stairs two at a time, "Stacey says she uses her tablet mostly for school, but also plays games. I'm in luck. Maybe we can be partners and play in the Nationals."

"How do you do that?"

"We have to play games already created and get a good score. And also design a game of our own. That will be the hard part."

Enthused, he went on. "I'll pick a game for Stacey and me to play. We can do it over and over and figure out how it was constructed and then how to construct one of our own."

Intrigued, Marv asked, "How do you win anything that way?"

"No, not that way. To win we have to get a high score on a game already being played by hundreds around the world."

"Don't forget, anything you send to Stacey will be censored at the prison. Be careful. Don't get her in trouble."

"Don't worry."

Later that month Marv decided to join Bobby at the Gamers' Convention in Chicago. He could keep an eye on him, a short twelve-year-old kid in among professionals might appear to be a kid who could be exploited. Marv would stay in the background to help Bobby just in case.

He needn't have worried. He could spot Bobby, making his way around the huge convention floor, asking gaming questions, as for instance, how to figure out the platforms of certain games. He sat in open discussions on coding, and in discussions about the best way to create check-points for the game he was creating.

At first his questions to the gamers were passed over, until he was recognized as fairly knowledgeable.

One man maybe in his late twenties, took notice of Bobby and started a private conversation with him. Marv stood close by, though he couldn't hear the conversation, he saw the man give Bobby a business card before they separated. Bobby explained to his father, "He gave me his email and said to contact him if I wanted to share what I was doing. Said he'd be interested in the game I was working on. Maybe he could help me, and he said maybe he could help me sell it when I finished it." Bobby laughed, "*If* I ever finish it."

"Where's he from?

Bobby looked at the card. "Some place in Wisconsin. They're from all over."

Marv had more questions, but they could wait. He was proud of his young son, so grown up, but only twelve-years old. Bobby was learning a whole new language of sorts, spread out as games, but evolving as something which players had to decipher.

Marv felt a little left-behind, as when there were all those violent computer games so popular when computer games first hit the market and blamed for the country's violence, but now barely played, the more subtle goals more appealing.

Pleased with Bobby for learning all this by himself, Marv would tell him of his pride on their trip back to Evanston.

MARV AND KAREN

On one of the nights after Adele had fallen asleep, Marv crept downstairs to use the phone in the study.

"How are you doing?" He asked his usual question of Karen.

"Oh, I'm okay. Surviving. Missing my boys, Charlie and Josh."

"What do you do with your time?"

"Been meeting with my old bridge group. Women I've known for years but haven't seen since Josh's funeral. Trying to keep what sanity I have."

"Karen," Marv asked hesitantly, "the kids and I are going to see Stacey the week-end after this. Any chance you'd consider going with us."

"Yes," Karen answered immediately. "I'd love to. Stacey is the closest person to Josh there is."

"I was going to ask you before, but I thought it might be hard for you. Stacey may remind you too much..."

"No. That's what would be good. Seeing Stacey would keep Josh alive for me."

When Marv told Maggie and Bobby that Karen would be joining them on their next visit to Stacey, Bobby said, "Cool."

Maggie asked, "Would she sleep in the bed with you, Dad. All in the same room.?"

"No, Hon. She will have a separate room."

"Does she know Stacey?" Bobby asked.

"Yes. Of course. Stacey was at Josh's house often."

"Same as Josh was here all the time," Maggie offered.

"Why did he have to go and kill himself? He was such a neat guy," Bobby said. Marv let the question die. How could he answer a question like that?

He didn't know how he would tell Adele about Karen going with them to see Stacey, but he didn't have to consider that for long as Maggie blurted out that news at dinner the next night.

Adele was taken aback for a moment and then squared her shoulders and said she thought that was a good idea, that it would be good for Karen. Nothing more was said though Marv's thinking about the trip filled him with apprehension.

How would he feel sitting next to Karen for the three hour plane ride? How awkward would it be getting plane tickets with a woman having another name, or motel rooms for all, except one person in another room? But what he could not imagine was how Stacey was going to react when she saw the woman in their group was not her mother.

But like so many of his worries recently, his children seemed to take the helm and dissipate the awkwardness he had anticipated. After their security clearance at the prison, when the four walked into the visitors' room and approached the table where they saw Stacey sitting, the situation was so comfortable, it was as though everything was as expected.

Stacey got up and ran across the room to her family, hugging each in turn and then melted into Karen's arms, both sobbing tears they had needed to shed together for almost a year.

Words were not necessary, were in fact unwelcome. This was a private connection of two people who loved the same person, now sharing that love with each other.

Bobby wondered, but did not ask, why nobody spoke of Josh. Isn't that why Karen came?

Marv noticed that Maggie became moody when she couldn't get Stacey's attention as she usually did. She whispered to her father that all Stacey wanted to do was to hold Karen's hand. Bobby had more luck. Stacey was all ears when he talked about the game he was designing that required her tech expertise before they could try to sell it.

After their initial considerations, Stacey told Bobby, "You need to get your art work coordinated with the music. Have you even got musicians lined up? Is Mike Lopez still interested? I think there's a lot more to do before we're anywhere near ready to look for a buyer."

"You know we don't have any money for that," Bobby told her. "But I have someone who thinks this game is a real winner. He lives in Wisconsin and we've been online. I could give him fifty percent and he could do some of the business work. Dad's been helping me communicate with him. His name is Dale."

"I hope he's not just some scammer, Dad. What do you know about him? Hope he's not exploiting Bobby, and going to make off with our game."

"I'm having him checked out on line before Bobby goes any further with him. So far not much information on him because gaming is so new."

Bobby tried to limit the talk about Dale. "He's a neat guy, Stace. Knows gaming backwards and forward."

"Bobby, you think everybody's a 'neat guy'," Stacey cautioned him. "Don't make any deals with Dale without Dad's okay. A minor can't make a contract, so I guess I don't have to worry. But slow down, Bobby. We've still got a lot of work to do before we think of selling."

When she saw Bobby's dejected look, she gave him a boost. "I've got the dialogue for the Yaddis' meeting, so all you need now is to finish the art work. I'll send you the dialogue in about a week."

All three, Stacey, Bobby, and their father were amazed how Stacey's upcoming Business Degree fit into Bobby's interest in designing an internet game. Marv was especially amazed how Stacey, who had never had a serious conversation with her "bratty brother," was now even deferring to him on occasion for advice in how best to coordinate the design, conversation, and music. This could not have happened, he realized, if prerequisites for college degrees in Business in most colleges and universities had not begun to include Advanced Computer Technology which include Computer Gaming.

Very little of the course contents were new to Stacey, having been a "computer nerd" since grammar school. It was about the only study she could pursue that didn't include any input from her mother who refused to learn "all that mumble jumble."

With the growth in gaming in just a few years from child's play to business models, in designs, CEO's represented by battling dinosaurs or battleships were pitted against each other in life or death maneuvers, not based on morality of good and evil, but on ever-increasing subtle forms of intelligence.

Whatever Stacey had subconsciously repressed in her years of playing her mother's surrogate, erupted in her enthusiasm for technologically projecting Bobby's design onto the computer screen. Combined, Stacey, Bobby and Maggie had long ago exceeded whatever computer help their father could give them.

About a month after Dale gave Bobby his business card in Chicago, Marv contacted Dale, identified himself, telling Dale he would be looking for an agent to represent his children in putting their game up for auction. First he had contacted Stacey's attorney to set up a corporation, and with his children's consent, established himself as president and sole owner, aware that property developed by prison inmates became prison property, Stacey's name was purposely omitted from the legal papers though there was an unwritten agreement between Stacey and Bobby which would be forever honored.

As the brother and sister worked to join computer technology with game design, Stacey often mused to herself about Josh, knowing how helpful he would have been with this work. She remembered how, long ago, Bobby was thrilled when Josh bought Bobby that first computer, though Bobby was still in elementary school. She remembered how Bobby, right away, began drawing and then transferring his drawings to the computer.

Still musing unrelated to computers, but thinking of Josh, Stacey told Karen about the baby born in the prison to her friend, Ava. She was thrilled to tell Karen she named the day-old baby "Josh", before it had been taken to Child Protective Services.

When Karen was told, she shook her head, not comprehending. How could Stacey name someone's else's baby? Stacey explained further and watched the transformation on Karen's face.

"Could I find this baby?" Karen asked, hesitantly.

"I don't know, but I could find out," Stacey said.

Unexpectedly Karen hugged Stacey. "You're so different," Karen said kissing her on the cheek.

"Though I saw you often when you were with Josh, I don't think I ever knew you."

Stacey pulled back, looking at Karen as though searching for something. "I *am* different," she said in a studied voice. "I *feel* different. I never felt so free before."

KAREN

On the long trip home from prison that afternoon, each of the four, Marv, Bobby, Maggie, and Karen were silent most of the plane ride, working through their private thoughts. Marv reminding himself to check with his attorney to get the Dale Casey's corporation papers in order. Maggie trying to dispel the gloom of not having been able to get close to Stacey, Bobby mentally playing his game to search out flaws, Karen anxious to explore the possibility of finding the baby 'Josh', yet not making any mental plans if she did find him.

Could she adopt the baby? She didn't know why she was obsessing about this. Is this, she asked herself, what her husband Charlie went through before he lost his hold on reality? Maybe she should make an appointment with the psychiatrist who had explained Charlie's condition to her.

Sitting next to Marv, their arms touching on the arm rest, she felt Marv's hand cover hers. She looked at him and saw something she hadn't seen or recognized before.

He held contact with her eyes. They both recognized they were no longer just friends. She slowly put her hand in her lap, unable to sort her feelings of excitement she had not felt in years.

Once in Evanston, carrying her suitcase to Karen's door, Marv wanted to hold Karen to him, but dared not, being conscious of his children watching from his car.

At their home, Maggie and Bobby were preoccupied and unable to give their mother much attention when she asked questions about Karen and Stacey. Marv gave Adele a perfunctory kiss and carried his suitcase upstairs. Once he sat on his bed and held his head in his hands, unaware for some time that his palms were wet with his tears.

Karen, immobilized for months by the death of her only child, awakened the next morning with a renewed purpose for her life. She would search for the baby born in Stacey's prison named Josh who would be in some foster home, and learn if she could adopt him. No need to have any discussion about this with her husband, Charlie, who had no connection anymore to reality. This would be her sole search, and, she realized, it would be one of the few times she would have any significant influence, however symbolically, on Josh's life.

Rather than a phone call to the Child Protective Office, Karen believed her physical presence, her appearance of stability would be most persuasive to balance the negative of her older age, which she believed would be the only drawback to her success in getting adoption approval. When she was asked her birth date and age she answered, "forty-five."

"Health?'

"Good. Should I bring a doctor's report?"

"Not yet. Let's get through this first phase to see if we should continue."

"Yes. Of course." Karen tried to display a confidence she didn't feel.

"Any children?"

"Yes."

"Sex and age?"

"Twenty-three. Male."

"His current address."

"He is dead."

The interviewer put down her pen and looked at Karen who was weeping, silently .

She tried consoling herself that this had been a crazy idea anyway. It was wild of her to think this could happen.

The interviewer, unrelated to the questionnaire on her desk, but hoping to mitigate Karen's crying, asked, "How did he die?

"He killed himself."

"Oh, My! Do you know why?"

"Yes. I am told he was raped."

Aghast, the interviewer asked, "Where?"

"In prison."

The interviewer wondered if she should continue these questions. "Why" she asked, "was he in prison?"

Without a sob and almost in a whisper, Karen said for the first time, "He killed his baby."

Karen stood up, left the room, left the building, in a daze, found her car in the parking lot, and drove to her home. She felt strangely unburdened about her son's crime, or was it her husband's crime, imposing his need to play football onto his son, who practiced all his young life so his father could achieve *his* dream, vicariously.

Though she knew what was happening with Josh, she rationalized that Josh accepted what was laid out for him. He did not protest, loved football, and he seemed to be a happy boy.

MAGGIE

Except for the necessities of child raising, Adele had little time for Maggie while Stacey was living at home. When Marv realized Adele was changing her focus from Stacey to thirteen-year-old Maggie, he did what he could to give Maggie the freedom she had previously enjoyed.

It was a struggle between the parents, with Adele making arrangements for beauty pageant trips, escorting Maggie with her suitcase of flouncy dresses, make-up, and wigs, contrasted with Marv's endless arguments to cut down on such "nonsense" for his younger daughter, who would rather abscond with her brother's skateboard without his knowing it, to the city skateboard park.

There she would be, the only girl with a pack of boys her age, free in her torn levis, dull-colored tank tops, with her short hair slicked back and tied in a pony tail to keep it from getting in her eyes.

Maggie learned to whip the skateboard in time to make an almost impossible downhill landing as she steered it through the air with the alternating weight of one foot and then the other, making it land exactly as she calculated.

It wasn't long before mothers of young boys were bringing their small sons for skateboard lessons from Maggie, who taught "safe landing," and "speed regulation," as more important than twirling mid-air.

Was there some jealousy of Maggie from boys her age, for stealing the show at the Saturday morning skateboard neighborhood round ups? She didn't care. Even though this was a boys' sport, hardly anyone knew she was not a boy. She didn't hide from being a girl, she just didn't mingle with the others in the park.

Marv pointed Maggie to a newspaper article about skateboarding being considered as an Olympic sport. Unfortunately, she told him after reading the article, it wouldn't be accepted for the Olympics until 2020 in Japan, unless it was voted down by the sport's enthusiasts who claimed the Olympics tended to ruin some sports. Maggie didn't care. She would skate anyway, she told her father.

"Nothing makes me feel so free as when I'm up above the world and can control which way I want to go."

She never had to sneak Bobby's skateboard after that, because her father bought Maggie her very own board.

BOBBY, MARV, DALE

Uncharacteristically, Bobby, who more often than not, noisily interrupted his father in whatever he was doing, stood quietly by his father's side until he had finished that page of the paper. Aware of someone's presence, Marv looked up and saw his son standing patiently.

"Oh, HI Son. What's up?"

"Dad, I have an idea."

"I'm not surprised," he said, folding his paper and putting it on the floor.

"You pay Mr. Tanaka to do the gardening?" Bobby asked.

"Yes."

"How much?"

"Fifty dollars a week."

"Dad. What if I did that and you paid me?"

"I don't think so, Bobby. His family needs the money, and gardening is the only kind of job a man his age can find."

"But I would pay him. See, you pay me and I use that money to pay him."

"What kind of talk is that? Gardening is a physically hard job. You're not big enough to do what Mr. Tanaka does."

"What kind of muscle does it take to push a gas mower, or use an electric shrub trimmer."

"Why are you so eager to earn that money? What's up?"

"I want to learn Japanese."

"What? Why?"

"So I can go to Japan, maybe when I graduate from high school. No point going there if I can't speak the language."

"Bobby. Start at the beginning. What's this all about?"

"Well, you know I'm into games. They're the things these days. Not all that violence stuff, now, it's all about using metaphors that..."

"Yes. I know what a metaphor is."

"Okay... like they stand for other things and compete in... well the games are programmed for a deeper kind of searching and winning, depending on scores."

"I don't understand. Go back to Mr. Tanaka. Where does he come in?"

"It's easy. You pay me, I do the gardening, I pay him to teach me Japanese. It's all about the games."

"I don't think this is a good idea. You need to spend your time with school work and being a kid. You're going to work all your life. No need to start at twelve years old."

"Come on, Dad. Japan is where game programming, and hooking up with promoters, sales, all that stuff takes place in Tokyo. It's the world headquarters... "

"And you're thinking of going to Japan?" Marv smiled.

"Not right away, but eventually."

Marv wondered about all this. "Have you talked to Mr. Tanaka about this?"

"No. Not yet. No way I can pay him if you don't agree to this."

Still Marv said nothing.

"See, Dad, he could teach me the same number of hours he works for you, only instead of all in one day a week, it would be he would teach me one hour a day after school."

"You've figured this all out,... interesting." Never one to quench his children's enthusiasm, Marv said, "Give it a try. See what Mr. Tanaka says. Make no commitment without me. Okay? Get your figures and hours all in mind and even on paper. And maybe," he thought out loud, "get Mr. Tanaka to give you a few hours teaching you gardening. I want my lawns and shrubs trimmed as good as he trims them."

Bobby smiled, ready to dash out of the room.

"Good luck," Marv said to Bobby's disappearing figure. "By the way, Bobby," Marv called after him, "how does one learn Japanese? Do they have an alphabet? Are all those figures... does each line or whatever, represent a letter, and the whole thing, a sentence?"

Bobby answered, "Beats me." Then he turned to his father, "Hey Dad... Want to learn with me?"

"It's a thought. You take a lesson in the afternoon and teach me after dinner. That's a good way for you to learn." He picked up his newspaper and found the article he was reading before Bobby had interrupted him. Bobby skipped stairs on his way to his room where his cell phone was ringing.

"Bobby, it's Dale. How you doin'?"

"Dale? Oh, yes. Dale from when we met in Chicago?"

"That's the one. How you doin'?"

Bobby stumbled. "Okay. How you?"

Dale answered briskly, "I'm okay, Bobby. I'm going to be in Denver next week, over Memorial Day. Any chance you could get to Denver?"

Still confused, Bobby asked, simply, "Why?"

"Don't you get the Games Bulletin?"

"No."

"Oh. I'll get you on their mailing list. Denver Memorial weekend is always the biggest gathering of gamers other than Chicago. I'm sponsoring six other gamers under 15 years old for this session."

"Yes?"

"Interested?"

"Of course."

"Here's what you do. Get your dad on the line, or have him call me. I have to get parent-permission for this. I'll explain the details to him, or your mother. It doesn't matter. All these boys have expertise in one or two facets of developing games which I can help with, especially help with marketing if I think the games are saleable. But this is what I need to talk to your parents about. But first of all I need to know if you are interested."

"Yes. I'll ask my dad to call you. I have your card. Oh boy, this sounds good. Bye."

Bobby didn't want to talk to his dad about this idea in front of his mother, who would be sure to jinx it for any reason she could think of, if she even listened to it in the first place. But Marv was no longer in his living room chair, reading his paper. He had spotted Mr. Tanaka in his yard about to trim the shrubs, when he dropped his newspaper on the floor again and went outside. Bobby, watching that encounter, decided to postpone asking his father to call Dale until later.

"But he's only twelve-years-old," Bobby heard his mother speaking to his father, after there had been a long phone call from Dale to Marv that evening.

"I'll be there with him, as will other parents."

"How can you take time off from work? You're lucky to even have a job at this point."

"You're right there, Hon. I've been looking around, getting my resume up-to-date."

"You didn't tell me?"

"I didn't want to upset you."

"You can't leave me in the dark, Marv. What is going on?"

"Fred is keeping me on out of charity, but that has its limits."

"But you can go to Denver for a week with Bobby? What will that cost?"

"Nothing."

"Who is this guy, Dale? What's he want with you and Bobby?"

"Don't get riled up. He's a gaming expert, setting up a.... well, it's like those tennis schools in Florida. There are ex tennis champions who start schools for young children. The kids live on the grounds, in barracks I guess, take tennis lessons everyday for a month at a time and over the years they graduate from amateurs in their league to professionals when they start winning qualifying matches. The schools are difficult to get into."

"How does this relate to Bobby?

"It's the same kind of school Dale is setting up. He has investors who back the project, pull promising young boys into the school on scholarships. And when the students start winning contests for their various gaming talents, at Gaming Conventions, the students and the school share proportionately in the awards."

"Is this legal... doing this with kids?"

"That was my concern also. I asked attorney Mark Collins to check it out. He said Wisconsin state law has cleared and with certain restrictions, it is not illegal."

Marv thought for awhile, still not aware that Bobby was listening. "There might be a job there for me." He waited for a reaction from Adele.

"Like what? Will you become a gamer?" she smirked.

"He needs an assistant, one to set up his business structure. Might be a good thing to get in on the ground floor."

"You're serious?" Adele said.

"I should explore it. We didn't go into many details. I would have to learn the industry. We'll see. What do you think, Hon?"

To Marv's surprise, Adele answered, "I think it's worth exploring. It might be a way to help one of our children. One's in prison; one will not accept the road I am trying to lay out for her; the other is putting all his eggs in one basket, going God knows where. How long will this first trip to Denver last?"

"I think it's just a week - the first week of summer vacation. Most of the kids will be on trial, but Dale is sure Bobby will be accepted. He said Bobby was not just good for his age at gaming. He is good - period."

STACEY AND DALE

When Stacey received a letter in prison with a return address of *Casey International Games*, it was no surprise that the letter had been opened, and that some of the words has been blacked out. The writer introduced himself, explained his connection to Stacey's young brother and Stacey's father. Stacey sat on the edge of her bed wondering what her family's relationship to this stranger had to do with her.

Dear Stacey Hodgkins:

I met your father and brother, Bobby, in Chicago last year at the Chicago Gaming Convention and was very impressed with Bobby's understanding of the theory, and at such a young age. He, your father and I have been communicating since then. We may be meeting in Denver at the Western States Convention soon.

The reason I have taken the liberty of writing you is that I understand you have supplied the technicals of Bobby's game which is nearly finished. I have a gaming company and hope to include your brother as a member of this company in spite of his youth. I am wondering if I might meet with you to learn how you coordinated the technicals with game platforms, and other things. Of course I would expect to get Bobby's and your father's permission to acquire this before proceeding. But first I wanted to learn if you might be interested in joining my company in the technical support department. This could be done irrespective of your present situation.

If you are interested and would like to meet with me I will be in San Jose, not too far from you, within two months. Arrangements could be made for a non-contact meet on one of your visitor days. Not the best way to meet, but the best for now. Please check with your prison and let me know. I will look forward to hearing from you.

Sincerely, Dale Casey

Stacey wasted no time writing to her father, with a copy to Bobby, asking for information about Dale. Their return mails were practically the same, except that Marv referred to Dale as a pleasant young man, and Bobby referred to him as probably middle-aged. They both said he knew everything about on line gaming, though Stacey wondered how they knew he would know everything, since her brother and father knew so little. Anyway, she didn't see anything unusual in their description of what Dale did in his company. In fact Stacey was somewhat intrigued. She didn't know if she could be an employee of a company, even if only in an advisory capacity, while she was an inmate of a prison. She would find out.

She wrote Dale telling him she would follow up on learning the visiting-day schedule for the next two months, and the procedure for adding a non-family member to her list, which she had done when adding Karen's name.

She was trying to pull up imaginary pictures of the man named Dale, but none held in her mind. The only one that she could hold for awhile was a man of about forty, slightly balding, black hair, black-rimmed glasses and straight large front teeth. A true nerd as she had known in college.

Weeks later when a guard led a six-foot, young blonde man to the phone stall where she waited, she thought the guard must have the wrong visitor.

"Twenty minutes," the guard informed both Stacey and her visitor, as they picked up their phones and scanned the person on the other side of the separating, bullet-proof glass.

"New experience for me," Dale explained.

"Me too," Stacey answered.

"I wanted to meet you in person. I was impressed with the work you did with your brother on his game. He's a young genius."

"I really don't know how he compares with others. I just know he gets in and tackles the problem he sets for himself. He is the creator. I'm just the 'techie.'"

"One needs the other."

They searched for ways to keep the conversation going, but were also interested in assessing the physical presence of the other.

"Stacey, may I get personal for a minute?"

"Sure. No secrets here." But she knew what was coming.

"Your dad said you have a fifteen year sentence?"

"That's right." She never wanted to talk about her sentence. She looked down at her lap.

"But with time off for time spent in county jails you may be paroled in eleven. Did you find out if it's possible for an inmate to be employed by an outside company?"

"Yes I did, and yes that is possible if the company passes all the clearance tests, the inmate has been on the good behavior list for one year, and both employee and employer sign a contract with the prison with all the restrictions listed and agreed to."

"I see no problem there. I guess the next question is to ask if you are interested in working for my company? "

"Yes, of course. I don't know anything about it, but the timing is good because my degree work will be finished. I'm not sure what your company wants me to do, but I'll just wait and see."

"In the meantime," Dale told her, "I'll meet with my board. It's about time I presented them with a list of new employees and new recruits. I am excited for all that we can do. You will be a wonderful addition."

"Maybe."

"I will stay in touch, and will let you know when I come this way again." He hung up the phone, keeping his eyes on Stacey as she hung up her phone and walked away. Then he turned and walked toward the exit of the prison, already planning his return trip.

STACEY

Stacey, accompanied by a guard, returned to her cell, lay down on her bed and wondered what she was feeling. Her goal had been so focused on staying out of trouble with the guards, with the other inmates in her work-assignments, and keeping her college requirements up-to-date that she had not permitted herself time to day-dream. But now she comforted herself on her pillow, counted the squares of the ceiling sound-proof tiles, and gave in to her wandering thoughts.

Dale's looks, his voice, his business-like approach to his work and her possible affiliation with that work, made her aware of her physical being for the first time since her imprisonment. How did he see her? She hadn't washed her hair in ten days, nor made any effort to make it attractive. Always the first in line for the once-every -three-day shower. She was in and out as though it didn't matter if it was for cleaning, or just for feeling the water cover her body. And with the mandatory, orange jump-suits, there was no incentive or possibility for accessorizing her outfit.

After all her years of concentrating on her appearance, her walking around the house with a book on her head, the elocution lessons to modulate her voice, the countless beauty pageants from the time she was five years old, she realized she was, after four years in prison, not the well-groomed young lady who had checked in.

For a moment she regretted having had to shuck that person who was clean, always attractive, who stood straight with good posture, and spoke in lady-like sentences. What did Dale think of her? And why did she care? Could it be because he was one of the rare men she saw, aside from the guards? That he was bright and involved in the intricacies of on line gaming was surely an attraction. She was almost alarmed at her interest in him. It was like succumbing to a power over her, and not like her. Yet she continued to wonder.

DALE

Accompanied by a guard out the prison gate and walking toward his car in the parking lot, Dale found he didn't want to leave. Why had he been in such a hurry to close the conversation? There were still about ten minutes of his allotted time with Stacey. Why did he always have to be so business-like? When could he arrange another meeting? How soon would Bobby be ready for the tech coordination with his story-line, his animation, the final structure of his platform?

Dale didn't question why he was attracted to Stacey. Somehow he knew when he met Bobby and Marv, the third person in this equation would be the important link to a fulsome, working gaming operation. That she was "well-spoken," attractive, even though wearing prison garb, revealed something of her personality. And her finishing a college degree while in prison, spoke to her anticipation of the future, rather than taking an easier option of dwelling in the misery of looking to many years of wasted life. But why would he let any hint of personal feeling for someone in prison get into his psyche? A working arrangement was all he was looking for, one to pull Bobby's game along to a good sale.

Yet he thought on. How long would Stacey have yet to serve her sentence -- with good behavior? He figured fifteen years, minus the four she had served in jail. That was only eleven years. Eleven years!

STACEY

The more time passed after Dale's visit to Stacey, the more she missed him.

"That's ridiculous," she told herself. "We met for about twenty minutes, and now I can't shake the image of him. Sure I can do some gaming construction for him, but otherwise what would he want of me. Dad says he had to tell him why I was in prison. How gross! What a monster I truly am. Did I really... I don't want to think about it."

Stacey conveyed some of these rambling thoughts to Myra. "A woman who kills her own baby... nothing but a monster. Worse than that, I broke my promise to my mother, swearing on the Bible not to have sex before marriage, and then I hid breaking my promise by the worst thing ever."

"Darling," Myra said, "I've been here a long time and I've got a long time to go. Forever, actually. We have to make sense of our sentences or we will go crazy. And everyone here has a different take on their situation."

"I didn't get the death penalty" Myra continued, "which would have been the easy way out for both the prosecutor and actually easier for me, because without the State knowing why they gave me life without parole, what they did was to give me one final chance to restore myself."

"I'm working with Ann-Marie, the chaplain," Myra explained to Stacey, "she tells me the Bible says homosexuality is a sin. That works against my urge to be good, so I have to put the Bible aside, or else I am doomed just as I am beginning to like me. Maybe one day I can love me. There's one thing I'm disappointed in myself about."

"I can't imagine what they would be."

"Walking with a book on my head. Just couldn't get the hang of it."

They both laughed.

"I love you, Myra," Stacey said, "You are unselfish. You help me to look at myself without revulsion. That's hard to do, especially when I hold those newborns in the infirmary in my arms. How could I? How could I?"

"You were programmed from an early age. Remember what you told me about your mother and her Bible?" Stacey nodded.

"That she placed your hand on the Bible when you were ten years old and made you swear you would never have sex until you were married?" Stacey nodded again.

"And you had to graduate from college because she had not?"

"Yes. I know all that." Stacey started to cry and Myra hugged her.

"Don't forget, darling," Myra reminded her, "you're going to leave here one of these days and we cannot be together after that. When your parole board meets, years from now, you have to have steeled yourself to learn how to find yourself *by yourself...*"

"Myra, until I leave I will try not to think of life without you. You have kept me standing."

But that was before she had met Dale. Thoughts of Myra had begun to be replaced by thoughts of Dale, and thoughts of Josh were lost almost entirely.

MAGGIE

Maggie worked through the week's schoolwork to get to Saturday morning's skateboard gathering that started around eight, all skateboarders anxious to get their gear on and test their skills.

Sides were chosen and points decided on for specific tricks. Two attending parents and two skateboarders were the judges who kept score and the morning's skill testing was on, with one of the oldest, a boy about fourteen, who called the line-up. Maggie was not sure she would be chosen by either team because she had missed one Saturday, so she was pleased when she was the second one chosen by the team she preferred. She was anxious to show what she could do.

While her team racked up points for specific flips and smooth gliding to finishes, Maggie's team matched their points for superior "kickflips," "frontflips," and downhill strategies. When the Saturday morning competition ended, Maggie was chosen as the day's most valuable skateboarder. She walked back home pretending she had a book on her head.

Her father, Marv, congratulated her as she walked in the door, having heard the scores on the local radio station. "That's my girl," he said as he hugged her.

"You did well," her mother, Adele told her. "How long will you be doing this? You're going to be fourteen pretty soon. Maybe it's time to drop this kind of thing."

Maggie had heard her mother's complaint before, so she just smiled and walked the stairs up to her room, satisfied with her morning.

For all her stereotypically masculine traits, the constantly wearing Levis, hiding her hair in baseball caps worn backwards, her mother's feminization efforts did pay off in spite of Maggie's resistance. One never knows what lies underneath, or when it will emerge.

When her high school prepared for its annual "Mother-Daughter Tea," several years later, honoring graduating senior girls and their mothers, all junior girls were given the opportunity to sign up as models for the tea's fashion show.

There was no shortage of girls signing up when only ten were needed. Even so, Miss Robinson, the girls' gym teacher who helped every year with the fashion show, told Maggie she should sign up. Maggie smiled and was about to say, "No way." Instead she asked, "Why?"

"Because you have the best posture in the class. Like a professional model. You'd be so good."

Not used to compliments, Maggie laughed inwardly at the irony. Then she said, "Miss Robinson, I don't want to be a model, but I could help the girls learn to walk like models."

"Would you? Oh, Maggie that would be a gift. Every year it is such a job. The girls like the clothes they model, but they are self-conscious and awkward walking down the runway."

As the success of the tea proved, Maggie turned out to be a perfect tutor of how girls should show off clothes they were wearing, but also to portray themselves as professional models, which of course they were not.

When the tea was over, the mothers in attendance didn't talk so much about the clothes, as they did about the models, how poised and confident and professional they looked. They asked, "How did that happen?" They were just girls from the junior class. They were so well rehearsed. Soon Maggie Hodgkins' name was heard circulating among the students and the mothers.

There were three high schools in Evanston and each one held a Mother-Daughter Tea for their senior girls. And the remaining high schools in the adjacent counties got in touch with Miss Robinson at Maggie's high school to learn the name of the person to get her to help teach their models the art of modeling.

Maggie's reputation spread, not only to those high schools, but to other organizations around Evanston, service clubs and different charities around the city and even into Chicago, always trying to raise money for good causes. Maggie especially liked teaching girls rather than teaching women who were "set in their ways," and who did not like taking instruction from a high school girl.

Nevertheless, Evanston being close to Chicago, where service clubs with their perpetual money raising campaigns, found Maggie's name and cell phone number from the internet where she had posted a web page. She advertised her services for models, which was the inception of her modeling agency. She established and became financially solvent while she was just a high school senior.

While her mother was flattered that her recalcitrant daughter was teaching others skills that Maggie learned from her mother, her mother tried to stop Maggie in her tracks and get her back to mailing applications for entry to prestigious colleges to no avail. Maggie filled out the papers, but was bored in the process and never sent them.

She reasoned she could go all the way through four years of college and graduate to become the president of her modeling agency, which she already was. She answered her mother's questions with, "Not everybody needs to go to college, Mom."

Maggie who had been somewhat compliant with her mother's aims for her, to keep peace between them, with the growth of her modeling agency, tapered off her agreeable going along attitude which eventually evolved to, "No way, Mom. No more pageants. No way parading around on stages half naked, trying to win, 'Miss Illinois.' That's not for me. I love what I'm doing.

"It's not just helping people look the best they can, but I'm helping them develop confidence in themselves, encouraging them to practice some skill, like dancing, or playing a musical instrument, or singing, or acting.

"If they can't afford lessons, I can get them a sponsor once I see a spark of talent. It's no talent just to be pretty. They can't take credit for that. But they can take credit for playing a Chopin etude and raising listeners' appreciation."

"My, that's quite an explanation," was all Adele said, and never brought up the subject of college applications again.

Maggie's father, Marv, was overjoyed at her declaration of independence from her mother's domination, and the end of the squabbles. He was also surprised and approving of Maggie's web page, business cards and the results they brought, keeping her so busy she barely had time to get to her high school graduation.

Maggie was not interested in having a boyfriend. She continued to live with her parents who were glad to have her. She waited impatiently for her sister Stacey's release from prison, feeling sure she would return to the household where Bobby also lived, though he was off to Japan several times a year.

MARV

As Bobby grew from the short five foot little boy to the lankier five foot six, then five foot seven, and then eight, his mother and father wondered if he would ever stop growing. As a sometimes teen employee of Dale's "Bucking Horse" Corporation, he was one busy young man.

He kept his school work up to date, somewhat interested in most subjects, but especially interested in art as it would apply to his games, and mathematics as it would apply to spacing on his platforms. Unlike his sister Maggie, he had no interest in real-life sporting games such as skateboarding, though he would spend hours on the elipticle exercise machine, all the time working out his gaming problems in his head.

Marv, who had been promoted in Dale's corporation to Comptroller, frequently flew to Japan. Bobby sometimes accompanied him, Bobby being the one who had become somewhat fluent in Japanese as the result of his many years of studying that difficult language with the help of Mr. Tanaka.

On one of the flights to Japan, Bobby had to call the flight attendant to release the oxygen mask for his father who suddenly had difficulty breathing.

When the plane landed, Bobby saw to it that his father was rushed to the Tokyo hospital where his health was stabilized after lung X-rays were taken.

Bobby waited anxiously in the waiting room until a doctor emerged and beckoned him into his office. He announced, almost before Bobby had a chance to sit down, "Your father has advanced lung cancer in his right lung."

"Cancer?"

"Yes. The first thing we have to do is get him back to the States, and let his own doctors there take care of him."

Bobby cried openly, shaking his head. He then went to visit his father in the Intensive Care Unit not knowing if he should tell his father what he had just learned, but instead he learned his father had already had that conversation with the doctor.

Marv was sitting up in bed, an oxygen tube inserted in his nose. It occurred to Bobby his father looked many years older than he was. He wondered momentarily if lack of air did that to people.

"Guess we're going home Bobby without having that meeting with Dale. How do you like that? Round trip to Tokyo and back to Chicago just for a joy ride."

Bobby was aware his father was trying to make light of the situation, but his efforts just made everything more dire. He quickly excused himself, telling Marv he would be right back. He didn't want his father to see him crying uncontrollably which he did out in the hall.

He was relieved that people passed him in the hall, looked at him, and walked on, not feeling entitled to intrude on such grief.

Picking up on his responsibility, he called Dale on his cell phone to tell him of their misfortune and that they would not be able to put on a demonstration for the convention. Dale took command when he heard Bobby's voice as he said the word "cancer." Dale told Bobby to wait right there, that he would join him and Marv as soon as he could get away. "Don't go anyplace," were his kind orders.

Dale arrived at the hospital, hopping out of his taxi almost as it drove away, and running up the stairs, to find Marv's room.

"Don't make any quick decisions," Dale said as he noticed Marv waking up. "Give me the name of your regular doctor back home," he asked Marv who spouted off the name as though waiting to say it.

"I'll call him. You two save your energy."

Bobby was dumbfounded, having wondered what he should do. And here was Dale taking over for him and his father.

"Thank you, Dale," Marv told him. "I'd love to be home. I hate what this will do to Adele. She has no stamina for this kind of thing."

Marv continued, "Dale, I didn't know what a friend we had in you. I'll try to keep up my spirits just thinking of all you are doing. I guess Bobby can make arrangements for getting us home."

Not wanting to take anything away from Bobby, Dale reassured Marv that Bobby was up to that task and if he ran into trouble he was just to call Dale. "You have my number, Bobby."

"Marv," Dale continued, " I've been meaning to tell you, I met your daughter Stacey. You and I, we never seem to have time where we can sit down and chat, and now you're going back to Chicago."

"You met Stacey? How?" He almost sat up in the hospital bed.

"Yes. I went to Chowchilla. I arranged for me to visit her there."

"Why?"

"I wanted to meet her to ask if she would want to be an employee of 'Bucking Horse,' and if that was allowed for an inmate. It seems things might be possible."

"Well,..." was all that Marv could say, with a broad smile.

"Now in light of the circumstances I would like to get your consent for me to marry her."

"You must be out of your mind. Are you serious? Do you know when she will get out of prison? And you don't know her. Did you meet her more than once? This is..." he sputtered.

"I knew you'd think this is crazy, but I know what I want. Don't know when it could happen, but people do get married in prison. I haven't thought that far ahead."

"Have you talked to Stacey about this?"

"Good God, no. I don't want to scare her."

"Then what is this?'

"Marv, you know if you've found a diamond unexpectedly, do you just walk away from it? Or do you even subconsciously start to make plans in your mind about how to fit that diamond into your plans? To tell you the truth, I've never had an experience like the one I had, talking to Stacey through glass at our meeting. I shall see her again. We'll be working out some gaming problems."

"I'm dumbfounded." Marv was silent awhile, then, "Do you know how many years she has left in her sentence?"

"Near as I can figure her sentence is for fifteen years, she's served four. She has eleven to serve out. She is twenty-four-years-old now. People who think it is impossible to wait eleven years don't understand love."

"Love! God, Dale, you don't even know her."

"I do. I do."

"But why bring this up now? You've got eleven years."

"But do you, Marv?"

Nobody said a word. Bobby looked back and forth between the two of them, confused.

"I'm sorry, Marv. I am being selfish. I apologize. I want you to live to one hundred. Just want to hedge my bets on something as important as..."

"Of course I give my consent. I know this is far-flung, but you know how much I respect you, and if it comes to pass, how happy I will be. Unbelievable!"

Marv had put the idea of calling Karen out of his mind for a long time, but with this illness, he found he couldn't get her out of his mind. Several times he picked up the phone, rang her phone number, and when Karen answered he hung up.

Replaying the tape in his head of his unparalleled joy in Karen's arms, Marv's day dreams always concluded with disgust for a man who took advantage of a woman laid bare by the death of her only child. And not just a death - a suicide.

Tempted often to call and console Karen, Marv could not fend off the truth that made its way to his consciousness. He realized it was not so much consoling Karen, as taking his exquisite pleasure in her bed.

His better angels held him back until he decided he would not call her again. In the name of his wife and three children he would restore himself.

STACEY AND DALE

Whenever Dale could find a place in his business schedule to stop off at Fresno, California, rent a car, and drive to Chowchilla, he did so, having arranged with the Department of Corrections.

The twenty minute no-contact meeting was filled with five minutes of business and fifteen minutes of getting to know each other. The attraction grew stronger, as did the pain of parting. It was a love affair on hold.

There was also letter writing about some life stories, yet each managed to hold the subject matter within the boundaries of platonic interest. To venture outside their unwritten restrictions would put too much strain on restraint.

The months and then the years passed. Stacey graduated from the Business Department of Alamoza University, Colorado with a Bachelor of Science in accounting. Dale congratulated her, telling her she had established herself as a bone fide accountant in his "Bucking Horse" corporation.

When Stacey had five years left on the projected end of her sentence, Dale dared to ask, in one of their meetings, if Stacey felt she dared to talk of more personal matter between them. She hesitated, curious. While she silently wondered, Dale said, "No problem, if you don't want to."

"No," she said. "I think it's time."

Dale put his open palm on the glass that separated then and asked, "Stacey, when you are out of here, will you marry me?"

Stacey joined her hand to his on the glass, "Yes. I will be happy to marry you."

When they separated they each said to themselves they had never been so happy.

Stacey immediately wrote her family, then found Myra in the recreation room and told her, went to find Ava in her cell and told her. She then returned to her cell, lay down on her bed, giving herself to the joy she felt throughout her body.

A week later, a small registered package came to her, which was opened in the mail room and passed around by the clerks to admire. They had never had a diamond ring come in for censorship before.

The sergeant in charge of the mail room personally carried it to Stacey's cell. He let her put it on her ring finger before he took it from her for safekeeping until she was released .

She met the day with trepidation, fear that her parole would be rejected, and relief that prison would be over if she was granted parole. She was afraid she would say the wrong thing in answer to a question. Her crime was so horrendous she wondered how the parole board could look at her and release her. She almost convinced herself that she was defeated before the meeting even started.

She walked into the room and saw six people sitting at a long table, not recognizing anybody, but then, she told herself, why would she? With relief she saw Mark Collins at a table facing the long table, and another man at a table near Mark's that she assumed was the prosecuting attorney. She was ushered to sit next to her attorney.

She sat down and involuntarily shivered. The room was stark and overly well lit. The people on the Parole Panel were identified by the names on cards sitting in front of them for visitors to see. There were several employees of the Department of Corrections, one a Commissioner appointed by the Governor, and one a State Deputy Commissioner. Stacey was glad she was sitting next to Mark. She felt miserable, wished she didn't exist. She was glad there were no visitors.

She tried to warm her hands by sitting on them, but then decided she probably didn't look good doing that. She held them together on her lap and tried to concentrate on the words spoken by a man at the long table. Something about reviewing her crime which kind of floated past her.

Then a guard who had supervised her different jobs spoke and told the Board her work was always satisfactory and "she could be counted on." Mark stood up and brought the University Work at Colorado to the attention of the Board telling them she had completed her university work which she had started at Stanford University and now had a Bachelor of Science Degree, earned in prison, and had the promise of a full-time job in the internet world.

She was asked only one question to which she gave a short answer for fear of saying enough to get herself into trouble. She didn't want to sound muddled though her brain was not working in her favor. She was asked what she had learned in prison.

"To keep my focus on not getting into trouble so I could get released when my time was served, and I could get on with my life after my terrible crime." Then she immediately thought she had blown it. She should have said such and such. She was about to cry when the meeting was adjourned and disposition would be announced at a later date.

Over? Now all the things she could have said came rushing at her. She sat silently until Mark helped her up, a guard came to walk her back to her cell, and she struggled to find something encouraging about that meeting. She lay down on her bed and cried.

But weeks later she had to shelve all the negative feelings when she was notified that the Parole Board had granted her Parole.

She was told that if there was no change in her evaluation, in due time she would be returned to the county of her residence in Illinois at the time of her arrest, and that a parole officer from that county's supervision department would be assigned to her.

Her conditions of parole were outlined for her which included informing her that during her fifteen-year parole period her residence and possessions could be searched without warrant either by a police officer or parole agent. She must always tell her parole agent if she moved and supply the address. If she broke the law, she might be arrested even without new criminal charges.

That long-awaited day finally arrived. Myra and Ava were given permission to walk with Stacey and the guards to the prison exit gate. Without asking permission she hugged them all, including the two guards

Stacey, who had entered prison, barely more than a teenager, in street clothes fifteen years later emerged to embrace, for the first time, the man she would shortly marry at the age of thirty-seven.

She handed Dale the ring the guard has retrieved from the prison safe and given to her. He placed the ring on her engagement finger and kissed her. She was hugged by Maggie and Bobby, and then by Marv supported by his cane.

Marv explained to Stacey, her mother would see her later when Stacey was not associated with the prison. She wanted, she said, to have Stacey restored to her as the same beautiful daughter before she got into trouble, but not at prison gates.

Arrangements had been made with prison personnel before Stacey's release, for the family and Stacey's attorney Mark Collins, to meet Stacey at the gate and to travel to the family home in Evanston, Illinois. Mark Collins was responsible for Stacey's arrival in Evanston and responsible for introducing her to her parole officer before taking her to her home.

THREE YEARS LATER

It was a warm summer day at the Memorial Park in Evanston, Illinois, where several people sat on folding chairs near the open, grave-size hole in the green lawn, a casket suspended to be lowered into the opening. The minister stood at the grave site addressing the group.

"Dear family and friends of Marvin George Hodgkins, we gather to say our personal goodbyes to our loving father, husband, and loyal employee of Goldman Sachs, and for the past twenty-years, the vice president of Dale Casey Games Incorporated, 'Bucking Horse.' Marvin's son, Robert, has now taken that position."

"As the casket is lowered, each of you will be given a handful of soil to sprinkle on Marv's casket as you say a few last words to him, either silently or not."

I will read now from the most soothing of psalms, No. 23, as the pall bearers lower the casket. Please stand.

"The Lord is my shepherd, I shall not want. He maketh me to lie down in green pastures: he leadeth me beside the still waters. He restoreth my soul: he leadeth me in the paths of righteousness for his name's sake. Yea, though I walk through the valley of the shadow of death, I will fear no evil: for thou art with me; thy rod and thy staff comfort me. Thou preparest a table before me in the presence of mine enemies: thou anointest my head with oil; my cup runneth over. Surely goodness and mercy shall follow me all the days of my life: and I will dwell in the house of the Lord forever."

In turn, members of the group stepped up to the edge of the opening and dropped their hands full of soil onto the top of the casket.

Adele had been the first to rise and approach her husband's casket. She could not speak.

Bobby, over six feet tall, took the few steps, holding the hand of his diminutive Japanese wife, Mr. Tanaka's daughter, who stood by his side.

"Farewell," Bobby said through his weeping." I will miss you forever."

Stacey, married and newly pregnant was next, holding the hand of her husband, Dale. Overcome by the emotionality of her father's death and her pregnancy. She stood at the ledge of the opening, dropping the soil and looking longingly at the casket as she cried freely.

Maggie, five foot ten inches tall, in a three-piece black suit with a chartreuse scarf, approached and looked down at the casket as though she wanted to jump into it. She dropped the pieces of dirt slowly, her last goodbye to her father who fought for her freedom from her mother's enclosure and yet, in the end, partially endorsed it.

Stacey caught sight of a woman not part of the group, walking hurriedly to a private car and driving off. Recognizing Josh's mother, Karen, Stacey repressed an urge to call after her.

After thanking their minister, the mourners backed away from the grave and walked slowly over the lawn to the waiting funeral limousines.

When Stacey saw her mother holding back, staring at the half submerged coffin, not wanting to leave the grave, Stacey walked back to her, offered her hand to her mother who looked into Stacey's eyes, and then took her daughter's hand.

THE SOURCE

Ties That Blind is about an actual case that caught my attention possibly three years ago in a one-paragraph newspaper article of a young, unmarried college couple convicted of a crime that would spoil their parents' expectations for their children's future.

I wondered what the fall out could be for those who had gone through this experience, directly or indirectly. Beyond the newspaper article I did no research about these young people. The story after the crime is strictly my imagination of what might follow in the case of children trying to live up to their parents' unlived dreams.

The characters in this book are fictional and any similarity to people you know or knew is accidental.

June Stephenson
JuneStephensonBooks@yahoo.com

www.ingramcontent.com/pod-product-compliance
Lightning Source LLC
Chambersburg PA
CBHW032110280326
41933CB00009B/774